FINDING YOU AND YOUR DIRECTION:

11 WAYS TO FIND THE REAL YOU

TONI DOWREY

This book is dedicated to my family for the support they have given me in following my dreams. My mom, dad, sister, two daughters and my son. To my friend, Brent Duncan, for the inspiration. And to my husband for always being there for me.

INTRODUCTION

Sometimes we feel lost in this big thing we call life. We don't know where we are heading and we are trying to get answers to many questions. Sometimes we just need to be reminded of a few things to get us back on track. I have put together useful tools to get you pointed in the right direction. I do not have a PhD in the medical field. I am a motivator. Inspirer. Life challenger. I do not read about what to tell you. I live the experience like you do, and assist you to keep moving forward in a positive way. My life has taken a few twists and turns, and years of discovery, but I have learned much in this time to encourage others. I will assist you to reach your direction.

We all have our experiences in life. We all keep moving along, but sometimes we lose ourselves or lose sight of our destination. I am here to help you get back on track of finding who you are and where you want to go. We can change our mind many times of what we are looking for or life will change it for us. This is to help you keep your sights focused and keep you from veering off course and getting lost in the mess that may occur. I hope you find this useful but most of all that you always enjoy the journey!

Chapters

Chapter One

Finding Your Values

I am lost and can't find my way

Nobody here to blame,

Everything wrong and nothing right

My head holding down in shame.

I need to find who I really am

The person I am supposed to be,

Why am I here in this place of existence

Who really is the real me?

In finding who you are, you might find the unexpected. ~td

Have you ever heard or said: *I need to find myself?* Have you ever felt like you don't know which direction you need to go? Have you just felt lost? I don't mean driving somewhere, I mean lost in this big ole world. This book is going to get you in the right direction and assure you that you are right where you need to be. When we don't have a set direction, we can feel lost. When we don't have a guide, we may feel like we don't know where we are. But you are right where you need to be, reading this book. And getting back on the path you need to go.

People often say they need to find themselves when they are emotionally lost, especially after a traumatic experience such as a death, divorce, job loss, the end of a relationship, or an accident. They sometimes feel that their identity has been taken from them. They are no longer the person they were, and where do they go now and who really are they anyway? We attach ourselves to other people and things that define who we are. If we lose something in our life that provides this identity, then we lose ourselves as well.

Living without a person who has been a big part of your life can make anyone feel that a piece of yourself is missing. Where you went, they went. What you did, they did with you. Now doing things alone is not the same and it doesn't feel right. Even leaving or losing a job can bring these feelings on. That job was who you are, and now without it, who are you? Sometimes a person may simply be at a crossroad in their life. What they thought they wanted and were working towards isn't the same anymore, or it's so out of reach that they don't know which direction to go next. Maybe the sheer thought that you haven't been happy makes you wonder what you are doing here at all.

Maybe you feel lost because you think people know only what you represent as a job title, but not who you are as a real person. Maybe you are in the military and deployed, and while everyone else is living a "normal" life, you are away and not connected to the other parts of the world. Maybe you have too many obligations and no time for yourself to see who you really are. Many things can cause someone to feel lost internally. This is an uncomfortable feeling and very scary to most. What you *think* you are or should be compared to what you really *are* at this time in your life are not the same things. It is easy to ask the questions *Why am I here? What is my purpose? Why did this happen? Who am I?* So many questions you will ask and will most likely not get all the answers to. The unknown is a scary place to be when you don't know who you are or where you are going. But you don't need to continue to feel this way. This is not really living.

We all would like to be living a happy life, enjoying it to its fullest. Some of us are there, but for others it may take longer or we get lost along the way. My goal is that you are living a different life by the time you finish this book. You may not be at your peak of happiness and may not have found yourself quite yet, but you will be well on your way in the right direction. So, let's get started! No time to waste.

The first thing I want you to think of is why you feel lost. What happened to make you feel this way? Did you lose your job? Did a relationship end? Did you lose a loved one? Do you not feel happy with your current living situation? Are you financially not making ends meet? Do you want a change for success purposes? Write down whatever reason you have. If you have more than one reason, write them *all* down. Place them in order of importance, number one being the most important. Once the list is complete, go over your list a couple of times. While going over the list, if anything else comes to mind, write it down. When you are satisfied with the list, look at the reasons one more time and really concentrate on what you said and what brought you to the point of feeling lost internally.

How do you feel seeing these reasons on a piece of paper? They are now documented in your mind. Do you feel angry that something has so much control over you that you feel lost because of it? Do you feel relieved now that you have discovered what is behind this feeling? Just take a moment to allow yourself to feel whatever it is you are feeling. If you really don't know why you feel lost and you don't have a specific reason, write that down — it is the same as having as reason. You can still feel angry or relieved or sad or happy for not knowing what brought you here. Now, if you feel that you have soaked this part in, fold up the list. Put it in a drawer for safekeeping, and for right now, leave it alone.

The direction your life is going will determine why you feel lost. The most important thing to know is that your direction is based on *you*. Do not let someone else choose your direction for you, and do not blame someone for *your* direction changing.

For example, say you were married for fifteen years, and you thought everything was perfect. Then one day your partner decides to leave. Ouch! Now what? You were happily married. You have two, three, maybe four kids and a beautiful home. You were going to live with that person for the rest of your life. It was all planned out. You knew the direction you were going and now…it is gone! This person totally messed everything up for you! You don't know where you will be in the next five years, let alone the next month. Your direction is gone and now you are lost and blaming that person for messing up your life. Don't do that! (We will talk more about relationships later. I am just using that scenario as an example of how we sometimes blame someone else for our misdirection.)

Don't blame the partner, the boss, the landlord, the mortgage company, the loan officer, the doctor, the lawyer, or anyone else. There is no one to blame. *This includes yourself.* So let's not waste time on that. Blame itself can make you feel lost because you have no control when someone else has done something to or against you. But you can control your *reaction*. In fact, how you react makes you who you are.

You have the right to be upset when your direction changes course. Go ahead and feel angry or sad or whatever you need to feel. We are human, built with emotions in our bodies to use, and we need to use them. Cry! That helps sometimes as long as you know when to stop and not dwell in self-pity. Blaming will get you nowhere and is a complete waste of time. Remember that everybody has obstacles in their life at one time or another and usually more often than not. If you didn't have a change in direction every now and then, you would continue to be heading nowhere or to a dead end. So no more blame or shame!

If you feel that you have lost your direction, start right now to get back on track. For some it may be easy, and for others it may take a while. In any case, you have to start sometime, so why not start right now? If you don't like the lost feeling and you want to find your direction, then you are the only person who can turn it around.

The place to start: go back to the basics and look at what you value. Just like going back to childhood, when you were learning right from wrong and good from bad.

What you value will help you find who you are. Now you may be saying that you have no values, that nothing is that important to you any more, or you don't know what matters now. Not true! We all have values. We get caught up in the world, in our problems, in life, and in so many other things that we lose sight of what we truly value. We live and don't realize what we are living *for* anymore. Time to stop, sit down, and think about the values you were brought up with or have developed yourself. Maybe you value spending time with your friends. Maybe you value spending time alone. Maybe you value spending time with your family. Maybe you value working hard and relaxing or playing hard. Whatever it is, look at all the things that you value in your life.

Make a list of everything you can think of that may have the least bit of value to you. I know, another list! But trust me: you would not believe how much clearer things become when you can see them on paper, not just floating around in your head. So grab the pen and paper and make a list. Really put some heart into this, because this will be your base, your foundation, as you find direction in your life. The list may open up a whole new area for you, or one that you haven't thought of in a long time.

Then prioritize the list with most important first. For example:

1.   Family

2.   Work

3.   Health

4.   Pets

5.   Friends

6.   Relaxing nights

7.   Nights out

8.   Hobbies

9.   Volunteering and civic involvement

Your list can have one item or one hundred. Just make sure that you have them in priority order. Remember, the definition of *value* is a principal, standard, or quality considered worthwhile or desirable. Anything worthwhile in your life should be written down as a value.

Now that you have the definition of the word, recheck your list and see if you need to change the order of your values. What is the most worthwhile or desirable to you? After you have your list made, set it aside until the next day. Then look at your list again and make any additions or subtractions. Our minds are going so fast most of the time that we can shift gears in a matter of seconds. What may be of value to you today may not be the top priority to you tomorrow. I don't want you to be changing the list every day, though. The day after you originally make it, you can make any corrections you see fit. After that, leave the list the way it is.

We live our lives based on what we value, and that is how we know the direction to follow. I will use me in this example. Yes, I am only human, too. I was a single parent for ten years. Yes, I have felt lost at times, just like everyone else—but not for long. Because I was the sole physical provider for my kids, and that is one thing I value the most in my life, that kept me going in the right direction, even though I may have got sidetracked or took a wrong turn. When I looked at my responsibilities, I was reminded that I need to keep moving. I had to go to work to make money to pay the bills and buy food and clothes and pay for sports. I needed to be a taxi to my kids and their friends. Most of all, I had to keep it all together while doing all these things. Whew! It could get crazy and hectic. But I know I needed to be there for my kids. I needed to be the bad guy, the good mom, the listener, and the teacher. Most importantly, I had to *be there*. Putting the attention toward my children has taken the focus off myself. At times I know I had lost my sense of direction because I was going in too many directions. It doesn't take me long to get my senses back and get myself back on track. I'm creating a foundation for my children, and the rest will be up to them. Since my children are on my top list of values, my life was based about supporting and caring for them.

Some children do not get a good start and feel negatively about their upbringing. If you experienced this kind of negativity in your childhood, you can set your own values right now to head in a direction that is right for you. Let those negative experiences give you positive values instead.

Not everyone is where they would like to be in life. It could be that your job is not the one you want. Or you don't make the salary you want. You don't live in a neighborhood you like. You don't have a loving and supportive partner. You don't have a supportive group of friends or family. For whatever reason, you don't have the life you want.

There are many things in life that we want but don't have. You can turn this desire into an opportunity to change your direction and work for the things you want. It is very easy to feel lost in the world. It is a huge place and we are very small in comparison. But that doesn't mean we are not important or that we don't make a difference. And just because we are not where we want to be right now, doesn't mean we won't be there later. I have my values, but I lose direction. That is life—it is going to happen. When this does happen, just get back on track and start moving the right way.

Take out your list of values. If you have "time with friends" on the list, for a week, take time to go out with them. I mean spend real time with them. Dedicate your time by paying attention to what they say and how you respond. Focus on the laughing and the fun. Don't worry about work, your phone, texts, or your laptop. Take the time to really enjoy their company. This will also show your friends how much you appreciate them and that you are not taking the friendship for granted. Maybe even buy a small gift of appreciation for no reason. Wouldn't that just shock them? Of course, they will probably think something is up. But it is OK to do something on a whim just because you can.

If you have finances on your list of values, then focus on that for a week. Take a good look at your budget. Write down all of your bills and your income. See where you can put an extra amount into your savings on your next paycheck. Saving just a few dollars will really add up quickly and give you control, which will give you a direction to follow. And knowing you have money in the bank will make you feel great! Live within your *means*, not within your *wants*. Take the week to start new goals and habits with your money. Use coupons, look for sales, buy generic brands. Be creative. Always pay your savings first, even if it is only ten dollars. Something is better than nothing.

Maybe you value a spiritual life but have not been dedicating time to it. Go to church, worship by the water, read about your beliefs, meditate, or pray. Bring yourself closer to what you believe. Focus on feeling the spirit and bring your heart closer to how you are feeling.

Health is a value many of us have, but we often choose to watch television and eat a hamburger and fries rather to go for a walk and eat fish and a salad. If it doesn't make you feel good, it is not a value in your life. If it makes you feel good about yourself, it is a value. Feel good about your health and focus on ways to improve it.

Whatever your values are, no matter how many you have, focus on each one for a week. Bring it back into your life and let yourself realize how important that value is to you. We rush around every day. Be here by 10 am, there by 12 pm, don't forget this at 2 pm. And at 5 pm we have to do that. Whew! Slow down! Go back to basics. Don't just do a quick fix on these values. Set aside time each day to focus on your values and appreciate them as being a part of your life. These values give you a sense of who you are and who you want to be. They help define your being and give you direction. This needs to be known to you internally.

You may wonder how a pet may be a value for your future. You would be amazed. That pet may be defining your future. How many times do you come home after a rough day, and you are tired, not in the mood to talk, and you just want to be left alone? When you come home and a pet comes running, is happy to see you, and gives you unconditional love, it is a good feeling. When you pet your dog or cat, it calms you down. It has been proven that people who have animals are less stressed (even if the animal may cause some stress in your life). That pet is giving you a longer life span to go in the direction you want to go. Value that.

Another example: let's use family as your value. You regularly talk to your sibling by text or phone. You call your mom once a week. You tell them you love them when you hang up, and all is good. There is really nothing else you can do to value these relationships, right? Of course there is. Take the time this week to really let them know you love them. *I love you* are not just words when they are said with the heart. Family is very important and sometimes taken for granted until it is too late. If your family lives close by, offer to take them to dinner, or better yet, make a dinner. If they live far away, mail them a card. Everyone likes the surprise of receiving a card in the mail. And I am not talking just at Christmas or birthdays. For no reason at all, let them know you were thinking of them. Maybe handwrite a letter and mail it. We are inundated with technology, but why not handwrite a letter and send it in the mail? That says you took the time to write a letter or card, address it, stick a stamp on it, and take it to the mailbox. The personal attention you gave to that letter or card can mean something immeasurable to the receiver.

At the end of the week, write down what you did for that value. What did you do to spend time focusing on it? Did you mail a card, walk the dog, organize bills, and write out a plan? What were your thoughts about that value after focusing on it? Did it become knowingly important to you? Did you find out how much you appreciate that in your life, or did you find that it really wasn't as important as you thought it would be? Go ahead and make any changes to your list at this time. You can add or delete values or change its priority on your list. I also want you to think about how focusing on the values made you or someone else feel. Did you surprise someone when they least expected it? Did your dog get excited to go for walks? Did you feel burdens leave your shoulders? Did you meet new people while exploring your values? Sometimes all it takes to stop feeling so lost is to focus on things that are important to you. When you actually take some time to focus on something else, you gain a little of who you are and where you are heading. It gives you a sense of control that everybody needs in order to have any kind of direction.

Don't continue to the next chapter until you have spent one week focusing on each value. This is really important to help you find a direction. It may sound silly to you now, and you may feel like a student not wanting to do homework, but it will be worth it.

As you do so and always as you move forward, keep your values in your life close to you. Don't stop focusing on them just because the week is over. Let them become a part of your life. These values are what keep you going in the direction in which you want to be going. They will keep you centered and grounded on who you are. Now you are heading in the right direction. Let's keep going!

Chapter Two

Toxic People

All they do is whine and complain

Gossip from morning till night

Ramble on about this person and that

Always acting so bitter and tight.

They hurt my feelings and self esteem

And they don't even seem to care

How do I get them out of my life

There is only so much I can bear.

When being a part of a bouquet, you may just need to be a single flower.

~td

Now that you have your list of values and you have worked on each for a week, let's move on. I am sure that one of your values was not hanging around toxic people. Toxic people can really make you feel lost without you even knowing why. You may not even know that the people in your life are toxic. We deal with different people every day at work, home, socially, family, stores, businesses. Although you cannot keep yourself away from toxic people all the time, you can learn to handle your feelings and emotions around them and not let them control where you feel you are in your life.

You may wonder how toxic people can give you a feeling of being lost. Toxic people are people who bring you down emotionally or pull a lot of energy from you to make themselves feel better. Let's start with the obvious place for most people: work. We all endure the people at work who gossip. You know, the person who comes in on Monday morning and will say, "Hey, did you hear what so-and-so did this weekend? I heard she went to a bar and left with someone and she has a boyfriend!" Or "Did you hear what so-and-so did? I heard she really messed up that report but still got the promotion. That position should have been mine. She either has something on someone or ..... you know!" And often the people listening are just as toxic. The common response would be, "Oh, my gosh! I knew there was something up with her!"

So it goes on and the gossip gets bigger than life, and pretty soon everybody thinks this girl doesn't deserve her job and is sleeping her way up the ladder. This girl has no idea until one day she catches wind of the gossip and finds herself crying in the bathroom. Let me ask you this: were you the one telling the story, commenting on the story, or ignoring the story? If you told the story or commented on the story, then you are toxic to yourself and other people. If you ignored the story, then I congratulate you on keeping yourself from toxic people or being toxic to others.

But in reality, most of us are the people who comment on the story. Why? Because we want to belong. If you don't comment, then you are at risk of not fitting in or being the one talked about. Who wants that? So we give in to the toxicity. Most of us feel bad afterwards and wonder why we gave in. The problem is we continue to do it and feel bad, and sooner or later we feel empty inside. We then wonder, *Why didn't I just stick up for her*?

I have worked in environments like that and been a part of the conversations. I was upset with myself for allowing it to happen and being involved, but I did it to belong. The only problem was that inside, I felt horrible. I kept questioning why I did it. Why did I listen? Why didn't I stop it? Do I really want to belong with a group who talked about and hurt other people? Was I a bad person? What was I doing? I was really uncomfortable with myself and dreading going to work because I wanted to belong to the group, but I knew I wasn't a hurtful person, and I didn't like it. Or, maybe I was hurtful and didn't know it. It was very confusing and I felt lost in myself because I was battling with my beliefs. So one day I thought, *I can't do this anymore.* When the talking started, I just left it at, "I didn't know that," or I just said, "Hmmmm." I didn't feed anyone or give the storyteller power to continue. Even though the stories didn't stop, I did. I felt so much better about myself knowing I wasn't battling my values any more. I value other people's feelings, and I didn't want to be part of hurting them. I still belonged to the group, but I didn't engage in the activity. After time I would defend the person being talked about and support why things may have happened a certain way. That is a hard thing to do with people who gossip and channel negative energy to their benefit. We are around people at work more than we're with our families, at least during the day, and we want to be accepted. Wanting to be accepted is good, but you don't want to belong to toxic activity. You can choose the environment you will feel comfortable in, even in a bad situation. A lot of this depends on your attitude.

I also had a job where I did not engage in negative gossip conversations, and it put me in a position of being a total outcast. After that, I am sure I *was* the conversation. To be shunned in a small office because you will not contribute to toxic behavior is a tough situation. That can damage your inner confidence. It also makes the day tough to get through and pulls a lot of good energy from you. That is why I suggested making small remarks but not feeding the conversation. Not allowing the conversation to continue any further but still having a comment to show you heard it has a different effect. It keeps you in the conversation and but gives you control of how the conversation will continue, and most storytellers will not recognize the difference. To be an outcast at a job is a horrible feeling. It is like being at school recess all day but not having anyone to play with on the playground. Keep communicating with your co-workers, but with a lighthearted tone, and move on.

These are the times you are finding you and not even realizing it. If you find that being in these situations bother you, then you know you are going against your values—even if you didn't think you had those values to begin with. Those values are inside of you. Try to focus on what you feel and allow yourself to accept those feelings and go along with them. You will feel so much better about yourself when you follow what you believe in. It gives you control, and that allows you to find a piece of yourself.

If you find yourself in an uncomfortable situation, get yourself out. For example, if you have more than two people in the conversation, remove yourself by saying you have to make a call or meet a deadline. If it is a one-on-one conversation, then maybe agree to disagree in a nice way. Make a comment such as, "I didn't know that, but I am glad I am now aware." Just keep it light and offer an acknowledgement, so the person feels like you are engaging in the conversation but doesn't realize you are not feeding into it and are actually ending it. This will help you feel good inside.

Feeling good inside is the best thing you can do for you. You go to work just about daily, so you need to be happy in your environment and not allow toxic people to bring you down. It also sets an example that most people want to follow but find hard to do. This is your dignity. Don't set the standards low.

Of course, there are other toxic people in the workplace as well. Some you may just not get along with. Some are bossy and arrogant. In those situations, stay away from them as much as possible. If you aren't able to do that, just remember this: Their attitude is revealing that they are insecure with who they are. Trying to hurt others or put them down is only a way to make themselves feel better or get power they don't have. It actually makes you feel bad for them, knowing that they are so unsure of who they really are. Feeling bad for them actually might help you get through the day and deny them the power to hurt you. When they are thinking they are better than others and are doing no wrong, let it go. Internally they are only hurting themselves. It will not change, and sometimes you just have to accept the way things are and adjust. Know in your heart that you are stronger than they are even if you are feeling weak.

There are a few more toxic people who are not easy to escape from. Sometimes you may not even realize that some friends or family members are toxic to you. Do you have a friend who calls you for advice or complains all the time about other people or relationships? Do you have a friend who cries on your shoulder most of the time? Or do you know a negative person who complains about everything being wrong and nothing is right in life? These are toxic people. Of course, your friends will come to you with problems. That is what friends are for, to be there through thick and thin and help each other out in times of need. But friendship isn't about being whined to continually. Those people are draining you spiritually and emotionally. Sometimes even physically. This can be unhealthy and make your sense of self-loss worse.

I have had people in my life who believe nothing is good. They are not happy and nothing in this world will make them happy. Do you know they are right? Nothing in this world can make you happy. You have to make yourself happy. Being happy isn't a given; it is how you want to be and how you are willing to view things. Being happy is not handed to you. Being happy is a choice.

It took me a long time to realize that I was around toxic people. All I noticed was how tired I was after being around them. Physically tired and emotionally drained. I didn't understand what was happening. It took years before I realized it was the people I was associating with. It was quite a strange experience. It was like a light bulb just went off one day and I thought, *I just don't like being with them anymore. They are bringing me down.* I tried an experiment: not talking to a certain person as much, keeping contacts and conversations short. Soon, I was feeling much better. I wasn't so tired after speaking with them or being in their presence. I also felt better about controlling my actions and my life.

Knowing what I can control makes a better life for me. The impact people have on you and how you feel is a powerful thing. Remember peer pressure? You did things you didn't want to do just to fit in and be cool. Well, it still happens in the adult world, but on different levels. The difference now is that hopefully we can see it more clearly and learn to say no. Everyone can make a choice, so make the choices that are good for you.

The first thing to do with family and friends that may be toxic to you is limit your time or conversations with them. Remember that annoying and toxic are not necessarily the same thing. Many people can annoy you, and you just don't want to be around them. That doesn't mean they are toxic. Toxic people are actually taking something from you emotionally and spiritually. It is harder to set boundaries with family and friends because they are around us so much and sometimes they are hard to avoid. They also mean more to us, so we don't want to hurt their feelings by avoiding them.

Family is family. They drive us nuts at times. We love them and they are blood. Sometimes family can be our worst toxic relationships. Some people have parents or siblings who complain, put you down, be non-supportive, or constantly give advice. They can also be smothering or over-protective. Both of these situations can be toxic. You will end up feeling insecure when they don't allow you to be who you are, insisting you be who they want you to be. In either of these situations, look at your values again. Look at what you want to be around and what you hold true to. Over time—and it could be a long time—you will learn that you are you. No matter what your family says or who they want you to be, you need to be you (as long as you are not damaging yourself physically and emotionally. Then perhaps you should consider some of their suggestions). Many of us like to please people and want them to be happy with us, but you cannot please everyone all the time, and that includes family. You need to be true to you.

I didn't always do what my parents wanted me to do and as an adult, I probably still don't. I hold true to myself. Whether my decisions are good or bad, I am me, and I need to live with the decisions I make. This is how we all learn. I do, however, listen to their advice and ask for it when needed. Advice from family is important but being knocked down or smothered is not. Just hold on to your values and lessen your family time if your situation is toxic. If they put you down, shake it off and come back to who you are and where you are heading. However, if the situation becomes abusive in any way, such as verbal, sexual, or physical, seek professional help right away to get out of the situation. You should never be in a situation that is damaging or dangerous. That is beyond toxic, and you need professional assistance.

Limit your time with your toxic family members. If limiting time is complicated, limit what you hear. Don't listen to being put down or being smothered in advice. Know in your heart that you are you, and they are who they are. Some people can't be pleased no matter what you do, so take some things with a grain of salt. I know that is not always easy, but it's something you can work on. If someone is unhappy in their own life, they sometimes take it out on others. This is not right or acceptable. You need to remain true to you. Acknowledge that you hear what is being said, but don't let it hold you back. You can only do what you can do and as long as you are happy with yourself, that is the most important thing. Sometimes you may just need to consider the source and leave it at that. Remember the saying "It is what it is."

I have seen disrespect in families, including verbal, physical, control, and power abuse. If you are from or in an environment like this, do not let it make you into a negative person. You can choose to make it an excuse in life or let it make you a strong and successful person (success comes from within, not from the material items you hold). Keep moving forward!

Friends are difficult, but not as difficult as family. Friends come and go, and they're not stuck to you forever. We all want friends. They help us release energy, they are fun, and they are supportive. A few good friends mean more than a lot of acquaintances. I know a lot of people I would call friends, but I have only a few that I can really count on who would be there in a heartbeat, should I need them. These are the friends that will be with me for the rest of my life and not drift away with time. These are the kind of friends you need to surround yourself with.

What you don't need to be around are the friends who are negative. The ones who constantly complain and cannot find anything

35

good in their life, saying things like, "I just don't see why he doesn't like me. I can't do anything right. Life is so hard. I just need a boyfriend to make me happy." Or the aggressive friend who doesn't ever have nice things to say about anything or anyone: "That guy is so stupid. He can't even drive. I am so sick of stupid people." Or you might have the controlling friend: "You should really wear more makeup. It would look better with your sweater. Maybe you should wear a different color to match your eyes." You might even have the user friend: "Can I borrow $50? I know I still owe you but I will pay it back." Toxic, all of them!

Instead, try being around friends who bring you up and say things like, "Hey, you look great! Let's go have fun, my treat!" Who would you rather be with and spend your precious time with? Do you want to spend time with a toxic person who drains you and sucks up all your energy or with someone who is boosting your spirits and giving you positive energy?

It can be hard to make good friends and find positive new people to spend time with. Know this: you need only a few people to call friends, a few who give you good energy and allow you to be yourself with them, who accept you for who you are with no conditions. Only a few people are all you need to be in a good place with yourself. Don't hang around people who drain you and make you feel bad. There are so many other people in this world to be around. You only have one life to live, so live it with a great group of people who feed you energy, not take it away.

This also goes for relationships. If you are feeling like your identity is being taken away instead of being fulfilled, look at the relationship from a different view. If you are being abused, leave! Women can abuse men, too. No one should be abused mentally or physically. This is beyond toxic and should not be tolerated, ever. Seek professional help if this is your case and get out of the situation now. If you are in a relationship that is non-abusive but controlling, non-supportive, or empty, then it is toxic.

Your relationship will always have its trials. They all do because we are all different and have our own values. Sometimes this can be a completion of two people coming together and at other times it can be a non-ending battle. Differences don't make a relationship toxic. Just because someone doesn't agree with you doesn't mean they are toxic for you. That could mean you are just being stubborn and may need to look at a situation differently. On the other hand, if you seem to battle it out all the time and it turns to a war to prove a point, that could be toxic for you.

There are so many components to a relationship. You should complement each other's lives. We don't have to always agree, but we should be able to discuss differences and see things from the other's perspective. It is very hard to find a solid relationship in today's society. Relationships are like appliances: after a while, many people upgrade and get a new model. Don't mistake "toxic" for "work." Relationships are work. It comes from the deep part of your being to give yourself completely to another person. This other person becomes a part of you. Together, you become one. In tough times, good times, and everything in between. There will be difficult times, and may possibly be times you reconsider the relationship. There will be times of happiness, pleasure, and the feeling of completeness. You take it all. You cannot give up just because of a bad situation. Love is hard to find and hard to hold on to. If you have it, don't take it for granted. If you don't have it right now, remember that it will come.

If the relationship is more than just work and it is more like a struggle, then look at what's making it that way and whether it's healthy for you. You don't want to lose your values and your identity. Toxic relationships can be hard to detect, especially when you are the one in it. It can take years to realize the relationship is toxic, and it usually takes an outside source to fill you in on this. Usually someone will ask if everything is ok. They may make note of things they witness about the relationship. If they say this with concern, you may want to think about what is being said and consider if this is a toxic relationship for you.

Sometimes others won't even see it if it is behind closed doors, and you will discover this on your own. I was married to someone for twelve years who didn't appreciate me or what I contributed to the family. He didn't make it obvious to other people, so when we divorced, it was a shock to others in our world. This included my family. On the other hand, I dated someone who I thought was my future and I believed everything was great. My mom, being on the outside, noticed I was not the same person with him and I was changing in negative ways. I wasn't as happy as I had been before, and I was often speaking negatively. This took a while for me to see, and after the relationship ended, I noticed a difference in my attitude and slowly came back to the more positive person I was. Both of these relationships were toxic. I did learn from them and try to find the positive and move forward.

Even if you are in a toxic relationship and it ends, don't look at it as being a negative thing. Some people are just not meant for each other. When you end a toxic relationship (with a friend or lover), you will feel a little lost. This is normal. There could even be a grieving period while you transform your situation. It will not last forever, but do give yourself time to heal. Then take this as a learning experience. What did you learn? How do you feel? What would you have changed? What would you not have changed? Learn.

I would not change anything about my relationships. That is not saying I am right and they were wrong. I am saying I wouldn't change how it all occurred. I have three wonderful children, I am stronger, and I grew from the experiences. Although I don't like some of what I went through, I like who I am now. I am a little more cautious with people than I used to be and I really don't like that, but I'm not as gullible as I was either. I am not as excitable, but maybe that change also occurs with age. I am independent (sometimes not such a good thing) and I don't rely on anyone as I did before. This is good for me because I was a very dependent person, and now I like knowing I can live my life single, not relying on a man, and still be happy.

We are not the same, so this may not be your case, or anyone else's. We will all have our own experiences in life and lessons we will learn. But now I like where I am. And if I hadn't had those toxic relationships, I would not be the person I am now. You don't want to stay in a toxic relationship, but you don't want to give up on a relationship if there is a way to make it better for the both of you. You will have to decide what is better for you.

After reading this chapter, think about relationships in your life that could be toxic. Maybe you surround yourself with great people who feed you energy and positive strength. Keep them around you! If you have one or two who do not, including family, friends, or lovers, then don't let them drain you emotionally, spiritually, or physically. Lessen the time you converse with them. If you notice that you feel better, you need to end the relationship. If it is a friend who is close to you through other friends, work, or family, and you cannot end the relationship completely, then spend less time around them. This is about you, not them. This concerns your health and well-being, and you need to do what is best for YOU!

This will not be easy and will take some time in some cases. Do not give up. Do not let yourself get sucked into staying in a toxic relationship. Get yourself out of it and keep yourself out of it. New toxic situations may come up, but you will be better aware and not allow them to drain you. Allow a feeling of loss, accept it, and then move ahead. Hold on to your values and keep moving in the right direction.

You know the old slogan, "misery loves company." Misery feeds off negative energy. Don't allow it to feed from you. Positive energy also loves company, and it is so much better to be fed positive energy than to be drained by negative.

Finally, learn what made the relationship toxic to you. What were they draining from you? What parts of you were they taking? Each person who crosses your path in life has crossed it for a reason. It could be a reason for you or for them. You may never know what the purpose was, but there is one. This is true for both the positive people and the negative ones. Accept the purpose if you find it, and if you don't, let it pass. It may not have been a lesson for you, but for them, and you were the tool *they* needed.

My grandma used to say, "Sometimes we ask why. Sometimes we will never know why and then sometimes we will look back and say, 'oh, that is why that happened.'

Chapter Three

Love and Loss and Rejection

My heart is so broken

I don't think it will mend

I can't deal with the pain

I can't do this again.

Why does love hurt so deeply

It shouldn't be this way

I don't think I will ever find love

But tomorrow is another day.

The greatest love you can ever lose is the love for yourself. ~td

We have all experienced it once (or twice or twenty times) in our life. We love someone so much, would do anything for them, they are the love of our life and then one day, out of nowhere, they leave. We didn't see it coming (or maybe we did but didn't think it would really happen). The pain, the heartache, the self-pity!

The pain of losing love is one of the largest causes of someone losing themselves. A part of you is now missing. You are no longer complete. You are empty. You are lost. Why did this happen? What do you do next? How can you go on? This list can go on and on. You live it over and over in your head. You think of the good times, the bad times, and everything else in between. You beat yourself up mentally, your stomach hurts, your chest feels heavy, you cry or you can't cry, you can't sleep, you can't eat, you don't want to go out, you don't want to watch television, you don't want to work, and the slow depression starts to creep in.

First, I want you to know that if you really cared for the person who is no longer with you, it is going to hurt, whether you left them or they left you. This is completely normal and you shouldn't expect anything different. You are a human with feelings, and our feelings shouldn't be suppressed. Everyone deals with the loss of love in their own way. Some people stay very busy, some take time to be alone, some move on quickly to the next person, some just don't ever get over it. We are all made up with different chemistry and none of us are the same. You need to deal with it in your way. But you need to deal with it.

If the relationship ended in an angry or bitter way, do not let that anger out on them or others in a harmful way. Yes, being cheated on is devastating. The anger you feel is set at rage. You are mad, hurt, confused, and mostly you want to take it out on the person they were with and the person you trusted to be faithful to you. But don't! It is not worth it in the long run. It might give you a sense of false vengeance, but really, just let it go. Instead, find another outlet such as a hard exercise session, a talk with a friend, or seek counseling, but hold your values and your dignity. Remember, how you act with regard to what has happened defines who you are.

Feeling the loss and all of a sudden being alone can paralyze anyone. What do you do with your time now? How do you make the pain go away? Will you ever find someone right for you? This can happen with a three-month relationship or a twenty-year marriage. Many couples who have been married for fifteen or twenty years are divorcing. People don't seem to work together anymore and they don't take the effort to make it work. The divorce rate is very high in this country, and to find someone who does not have baggage makes it difficult to find a future lasting relationship. Or so it seems.

You have to take baby steps to get over the loss of love. The pain doesn't just go away one night when you are sleeping, although that is what we would like to happen. Look back at the relationship and see what problems may have been there. There usually is more than one problem, and usually both people played a role. You also have to look at yourself and not just the other person. Of course we don't want to admit it, but the only way to move on is to confront our problems as well.

I had a relationship that ended in a hurtful way. We both had issues. I had a wall up to protect myself and it kept me from moving forward. He wanted someone there all the time and was moving too quickly for me. When the relationship ended, he was with another person within a couple days. (Or maybe before it actually ended; I am not sure.) I just know I went to the mall, which I hardly ever do, because I kept thinking of him and needed to get out of the house. It was at the mall that I saw him holding the hand of another woman. Just like that! He had moved on to the next girl. To know I could be replaced so quickly was like a knife stabbing my heart with a little twist to top it off. When someone tells you they love you and you are the person they want to be with, and then suddenly can find another woman to replace you, ouch! Then he wanted to be friends. Friends? Don't even go there, people.

I admit that I still have friendships with some people I have dated. Not everyone can be friends after a relationship. With pain like that, sometimes it is better to just let go. When you continue to communicate, sometimes it just makes it worse, and the pain doesn't completely heal. If you get along better as friends, then friendship is allowed. Otherwise, the friendship option is not an option so you can move on.

But for me, I had a hard time dealing with the loss and the fact he was with someone right away. I know I had some issues in the relationship. I didn't give him time that he deserved. I didn't allow my heart to be fully open to the relationship. I wouldn't sacrifice in some areas that I probably could have—actually, in ways I *should* have. He wanted someone around much of the time. I had been married for twelve years and single for six years, and I had become very independent. It was hard for me to share my time right away. I still had my guard up from being hurt from my divorce. I had been in an off-and-on relationship after my divorce, and I was still grieving from the loss of that relationship. All in all, although we were not meant to be together, that didn't make the breakup hurt any less.

So what did I learn from all of this? If I really love the person, I need to show them more often how I feel. Assuming a person knows is not healthy for a relationship: love needs to involve words and actions. I learned I need to make some sacrifices and not be so stubborn. I do not have to change who I am or change my values, but making *some* changes and sacrifices is very important in having a healthy relationship. I really don't think he learned anything, though, because the last time I talked to him (three years after we broke up), he still feels he did nothing wrong. He considered meeting his next girl to be "unplanned." That relationship, unplanned or not, did not work out for him. It took me a long time, but I did hold a friendship with him, and I honestly wish him the best, as I do with anyone from my past. Not everyone is meant to be together. That is why we date: so we can find the person who is right for us. Even if people marry, they may find they are not lifelong partners, but still learn from it all. Don't waste that time you had.

When you've lost a relationship, you've lost more than a person in your life. You also lost time, a partnership, feelings, parts of your heart, and normal activities. You lost so much that your brain just cannot comprehend it all at one time and you can feel lost. Your direction has to change, but when your direction is forced to change, which way do you go? Where do you start?

To start, feel the pain and loss. Accept that this hurts and it will for a few days, weeks, or even months. But not for years, because that is way too long and you need to move on with your life. It is not worth putting yourself through that. The only loss that you should feel for years is a death, and even then, at some point, you must move on. You need to accept the pain. You are human and this loss is going to hurt. Cry, mope, and even eat a container of ice cream. I suggest you do not hit anything, yell at anyone, drive recklessly, or use any kind of substance (except the ice cream) to fix your problem. Those behaviors are destructive and will only make matters worse in the long run. So be strong and deal with the pain in a constructive way. Go for walks, play with your dog or cat, call someone, write a journal, do some kickboxing or anything else that will release energy in a healthy way. Sometimes a few tokens at a batting range can do you some good.

When the pain starts to lessen, you can reflect back on the relationship in a more constructive manner. Have you realized what you learned? You should learn something from every experience you have, or you will repeat it over and over in future relationships until the lesson is learned. Even if you didn't realize that there was a problem, later you will come to see what could have been done differently. Some relationships can be taken for granted. Other relationships can just be comfortable, and it is too scary to step out of that zone. Yet sometimes, there is no excitement, and things become routine. People can only live like that for so long before they decide they want something more in a relationship. That is usually when the trouble begins. We want excitement, adventure, and love. When those things wind down, we sometimes seek them elsewhere. This can lead to straying, hanging out with friends more, or secluding yourself from the situation. Looking back to your past relationships, do you see any of these things?

Take a little time to reflect on this. Be constructive in your thoughts. Be honest with yourself. Hold yourself accountable in areas that you had responsibility. The only way for you to get into a new, healthy, and long-lasting relationship is to learn from your past ones. When thinking of what may have gone wrong, do not punish yourself. Do not wonder….. if only I did this or why did I do that. If I only would have or I should have. Don't beat yourself up. This is not a punishment. Learn and move on. Not all relationships are meant to last, some are meant to be learning tools. Take your experience on to the next person who may be "the one."

Now that you have gone through some grieving and you are learning from your experience, what do you do with yourself now? This will sound like a cliché, but it is true: keep yourself busy. Start or re-start some hobbies, exercise (this will not only help relieve stress but will also keep you looking good!), take a little getaway, go out with friends. And if you are ready, go on a date so you can get out there and not put yourself in a bubble that says "I am hurt and wounded. Stay away from me."

We all have our time to heal. The hurt doesn't go away completely for a while, but life does go on, and it doesn't stop to feel sorry for you. Your friends will be there to help you get through the initial part but after a while, you are on your own to get yourself back up and running.

When you have started to come out of your pity party, get back to living. Have fun! Laugh! Do things you enjoy and appreciate the people who listened to you and helped get you through. It does get better over time, and at this point you may even realize that the relationship wasn't as good as you thought it was. You may even discover that the person you thought you wanted to be with forever was not that person after all. If it wasn't meant to be, something will end it. And be thankful it ended because there really was a reason that person was not meant to be the one for you.

Now you need to reflect on you. You need to make yourself happy. Which by the way, is a choice, not a given. I mentioned that before. You can choose to be happy or choose to be unhappy. Most people think that being in a relationship is what qualifies being happy or unhappy. No. Being happy is being happy alone and then bringing that happiness into a relationship and sharing it with someone else.

Go back to your values. What is important to you? Has anything changed at this point? Is everything the same? Start taking steps to put those values back in your life. If you need to focus on them one by one for a week each time, then do it. This is your life. This is your world you live in everyday. Make it the best and don't let a broken relationship take your values from you, because it will honestly hurt only you, no one else. Do not allow someone to have that power over you. You have power to choose to hurt or move on. They are moving on and so should you. So, about those values: Look them over, focus on them, and be happy with yourself in a relationship-free moment in time.

Now, you still must know this in your heart that God has put people on earth to be together. What we want and what He wants may not always agree. Realize that there is a plan in place. You may not know just yet, and it is not for you to know, but you should believe that there is a person waiting for you just as you are waiting for them. Each person is different and must be treated that way. You can still remember the past and use it to help in your new choices. Your lessons, reflections, and values will get you off to a better start when you decide to take that next step again.

You may think that being alone is being lost. I think this is a time of being found. I learned so much after my divorce about myself. I also learned what I want out of life that I'd never noticed before. I was a very dependent person. I'd lived at home until I married. I married young and had three children while in my twenties. I had my parents, then a husband, then children. I never really spent time by myself. In the beginning of the divorce, I was devastated. I was very afraid to be alone, and I lived an hour from my family, which was a big deal to me. I was alone and I had to take care of three kids on my own. How on earth was I going to do this? How would I survive financially? How could I take on the role of mom and dad, work full-time, keep the kids in sports, keep up the house, and try to be sane? But I did. My children were all in elementary school when my ex-husband and I separated, and I raised them alone until my last child was a senior in high school.

They were tough times, but also the best times. The most meaningful times. They gave me strength I never knew I had, both mentally and physically. I was a mom in survival mode, learning what I had in me to get the job done. I found who I am and want to be. What was important in my life. What I would accept and what I would pass on. One of the hardest times in my life turned out to be one of the best times in finding more of who I was. Sometimes the best time to find you is when you are alone to focus on you. I will not deny that I still have some work to do on myself. I sacrificed much to care for my kids, so actually taking care of me is a work in progress. I have guilt when I'm pampering myself, but I am slowly learning that self-care is very important and guiltless.

Those times were also very difficult. I was faced with things I could not imagine getting through. Times of difficulties with the kids. Times where I just wanted to pick up the kids and move to some small town I picked on a map. But sometimes the tough times are where we learn the most about ourselves. We can learn about getting through those times alone rather than depending on someone to pick us up—rather, we can pick *ourselves* up. We fall and get right back up and keep moving. You will be amazed at how much you can do alone. The confidence in yourself at seeing your accomplishments will help you find and keep the direction you want to go.

I know people who cannot be alone. They always need someone in their life. They are miserable alone. Depressed. This is sad to me because the only person you will always have with you every day of your life is you. You need to focus on that one important person and discover how great you are alone. Then when the time is right, you can share that great you with someone else. If I had not been through and learned so much about independence, I never could have been in the wonderful relationship I am now. Ten years after raising my kids from a bad divorce and a few learning dating experiences, I met an amazing man in the military. During our first three years together, he was out of the country for two of those years. I moved to his home to care for his horses, and pigs he had given me. We also have dogs, ducks, chickens, and a little farm. My home was in a larger town and easier to rent, so I took the plunge and moved out and brought my kids with me. The farm is forty-five minutes from where I lived, and I would never had done this before my experiences.

The unknown is often scary. But even when we are unsure, knowing who we are inside allows us to go one step further and take chances. It is great to be able to accomplish these steps. Now I'm remarried, and this never would have happened if I hadn't stepped out of my comfort zone and trusted myself enough to take a leap of faith.

Find out more about yourself in your time alone. Where you have been. Where you want to go. Find your path and start walking. The only person who can make you stop walking is you.

What did you learn in this chapter? Just because one relationship ends, it is not *the* end. Learn from the relationship and see what brought it to an end. Put your values back into your life. Make yourself happy before you can be happy in a relationship. And you can be happy being single. Leave your baggage packed and put it away when you start a new relationship. Remember that there is a plan for you. You may not agree with the direction it is going but you are right in the place you need to be. Don't give up hope. Ever.

Note: Please remember that you need to be happy in a single life. Being happy is a choice, and you can do this being single. You will bring that happiness and appreciation into the next relationship. The most important thing I can tell you in this chapter is that you must always keep your own identity, even in a solid relationship. Your partner may complete you as a couple, but you will always be your own person.

Chapter Four

Life with Stress

This is too much to handle

I see no way out in sight

I feel so overpowered

I see darkness but no light.

I can't eat, sleep, or think

Starting to feel so doomed

If only I could get through this

And stop feeling so consumed!

The solution to the problem can be discovered from within you. ~td

Ahhh . . .stress! The little six letter word that starts with an *s* and ends with an *s*. Stress can be good or stress can be bad. Stress can make you sick. Stress can make you feel overwhelmed. Stress can make you excited. Stress can make you happy. Stress can make you feel lost. Job, kids, relationships, family, finances….. purchases, weddings, vacations….. the list of things that stress us can go on and on. Stress is a part of life.

Have you had the kind of stress that has taken you over and you can't think, eat, or sleep? Your mind is continually going and it won't stop. It consumes you to the point that you don't know what direction you are going, where to begin, or what step to take first. I think that most people have been there at one point in their life and most likely more than once. Yes, even me and more than once or twice. When change comes into our life, usually stress does, too. This kind of stress can take over quickly. Before you know it, you are lost and don't know what to do.

Just know that this is completely normal. It may feel like you are the only one feeling this way, but the person next to you could be feeling the same way, too. Just hang in there. You are going to get back on track and it will be one of those experiences that will make you grow stronger. Everything you learn during a trying time is going to make you connect to yourself a little bit more. You are going to find some weaknesses and strengths you didn't know you had. Just keep in mind, depending on what is causing the stress (relationship, money, work, etc..) it may take a little time to get through it. Allow yourself that time. That is the one thing that people don't do. We rush to move forward and we don't focus on where we are today. It helps to get through things by staying in the moment. Allow yourself to feel the things you feel and *really* feel it. Know it. Accept it. That is the first step to start controlling some of the stress in your life.

If you are scared, feel scared for the moment. Then focus on what is scaring you. For example, say you had a relationship that just ended. That can stress out anyone. Even if the relationship itself was stressful, this is a different kind of stress. What is scaring you? Are you afraid of being on your own? Scared you will not financially make it? Scared you will never find that "one?"

Or maybe you lost your job, in which case stress is an understatement. You are probably scared about not finding a new one, not making ends meet, or not feeling adequate. Maybe you just have a project at work and you are stressed about meeting a deadline. What will the outcome be? How is this project going to show your abilities to your boss or co-workers? Whatever the stress may be, accept it and feel it. Write down your fears and feelings. Write everything that comes to mind.

Go over what you wrote down. There could be only one thing or there could be many. Think about each stressful part of your life. This is where you can start to gain some control. Writing things down helps to bring them to life, making things real and helping you feel what you are feeling.

Start marking things off: Things that you don't have control over, let go. This part may be difficult because sometimes you're uncertain on what you control and what you don't. Just think of the items on your list and ask yourself, "Can I do anything about this?" "Can I change the situation?" If your answer is no, then mark it off the list. Some things you just have to accept and put it aside. It may make you a little more stressed knowing that you do not have any control over something, but it will help to know that it is no longer your concern. You cannot stress about something you have no control over. It is a waste of your energy. You need that energy to focus on what you *do* have control over.

Here is an example: You have a presentation at 7:00 am in four days, and this presentation can bring in important clients and a lot of money to your business. You want to make sure the meeting goes well. The right coffee needs to be ordered. Biscuits and fruit need to be served. The PowerPoint presentation needs to be put together. And you only have a few days to get everything done. You do not like speaking in front of a group, and the fear of this overwhelms you. The stress of knowing that your presentation is what makes or breaks a deal is a heavy burden. At this point, you can't even think about the coffee or fruit. It is all about the importance of the meeting. The fear of giving the presentation is so scary it's consuming your every thought. How will you get through the speech and not sweat, faint, or be sick?

Make a list for this situation. Take a few moments to list what is needed for the meeting, how long the presentation should be, and what food will be served. Example:

Presentation:

1.   Coffee – 1 decaf, 5 mocha lattes, 6 regular, 3 Italian sodas, creamers, and sugar. Order one day in advance for a pick up at 6:30 am.

2.   Fruit and biscuits – scones, assorted fruit, bagels, cream cheese, and butter. Order one day in advance for pick up at 6:30 am.

3.   PowerPoint – music, titles, pages and handouts. Fifteen copies. Have ready by 10:00 am the day before to review.

4.   Presentation – thirty minutes in typed format. Practice five times with a timer.

5.   Closing statement – no longer than three minutes. Allow time for questions and prepare possible answers ahead of time.

Look at the list and own it. Take responsibility of it so you have more control over the situation. Focusing on your list will help you to feel control and less stress over the presentation itself. It will help you to feel more relaxed knowing there are other items to go along with the presentation. Make sure you order the coffee and food a day prior to the meeting so all you need to do is pick it up and not wait. No need to add stress by waiting in a line and worrying about being late. Have the drink, food, and handouts ready at least twenty minutes before the meeting. Five minutes before the meeting, take four deep breaths. With every inhale you will breathe in calming, relaxing air and with every exhale you will blow out any stress you are holding in. Do this again a few seconds before the meeting. It has been proven that deep breathing calms the body and releases stress and anxiety. After the presentation, be proud of yourself and the job you did. If it went flawlessly, that is a great accomplishment. If there were some bumps, hey, at least you made it through. That alone is something to be proud of.

You can use this technique with almost anything in life. Some things may take longer than a thirty-minute presentation. Some things could take months. Just know that there is an end to the stress, although it may not feel that way at the time.

Let's look at something that may take months: finances. Oh, that money problem that most of us have or will have. This is a stress that no one likes to bear, and it can make anyone feel lost and out of control. You try so hard, work every day, and yet you just can't seem to be where you want to be or make ends meet. I have been there many times, and it ends. It may come back, but even then it will end again. I have written many budgets, many plans, but then things change and I start all over again. Whether you can't make ends meet or you want to save for something you can't yet afford, you can have some control in relieving some of the stress and the feeling of being lost.

Remember earlier when I said I have felt lost before but it doesn't last for long? Finances would be one of those reasons I would feel that way. What we can and cannot do, what we can buy and what we cannot, influences on how society sees us. People look at a broke person differently than they do a person who has a lot of money.

I don't want you to be one of those people who feel that way. And, yes, I have felt that way. Being a single mom for many years, I felt bad when my kids wanted something I couldn't afford. They would come home talking about their friends who took trips or had stuff they wanted. It was very difficult to not have the funds to supply all their wants. So I would be hurt and jealous of the people who were able to get what they and their kids wanted. It just made me feel worse. But it was wrong for me to be upset with others who could afford things that I could not.

Right now in the economic situation, many people are losing their homes or cars and filing for bankruptcy. It is a life-altering change. I have dealt with many of these situations at my job and talked to many people who are going through this. I feel for the people in that situation. I have said that everything is a learning experience and I have learned from this, too. I do not take anything I have for granted. I may not have a lot, but I have more than some. I may not have a huge house with a view, but I have shelter over my head. My kids were cared for and had food and clothes. I appreciate all that I have. I may have struggled to make a payment, but I had a home for my family to live in.

I have said you are happy by choice. This holds true in this situation as well. You can have financial difficulties and still be happy. I have talked to many people who have lost their homes. I am surprised by what I hear. There are some people who are angry and bitter. Their world has been turned upside down. They are forced to move from their home. The American dream is ripped from them. It is understandable why they would feel this way. I have also spoken to people who are still happy. A tragic thing has happened, but they know they need to move on, find a new place to live, and start a new chapter in their life. Of course they are scared and upset about the situation, but they are positive that new adventures lie ahead and things happen for a reason. They may have lost a home, but it is only a material thing. These people still have life, a future, and happiness.

These are tough times for many, and whether you're happy or not, it will be stressful when your finances are not in balance. Many websites can help you with a financial situation, and you can check out books at a library to get you on track again. When you start taking charge of your money instead of your money stepping all over you, you will gain your direction.

The first thing you need to do is set a realistic budget. Even if you have more money going out than coming in, you will still get some control of the situation. Make a list and look at any way you can cut back. Do you really need cable right now? Can you cut back on your cell phone? Unplug appliances while they're not in use. Make coffee at home instead of buying a latte. You could save $25.00 a week just on coffee. Make your lunch instead of buying out. Cut those coupons. Buy generic items. Carpool if you are able to. Try to run all errands during lunch hour or on the way home to cut back on driving. Those are just a few suggestions. Anything helps and adds up, even if it seems minor.

If you are way over budget, then you'll need to look at many more options. Get rid of your credit card balances, for one. Those need to get paid off and not used! Look at transferring the balance to one with a lower interest rate. If the option is available, look at trading in your car for a less expensive payment. Seek financial counseling if this is something you cannot do on your own.

You have options, but you need to discipline yourself. This is where you have the control. This is where you find your strengths and your weaknesses: what you can limit, what you can change, and what you are willing to do. This is hard. I have had many budgets that were tight. What are you willing to sacrifice? I would not sacrifice cable TV. To me, it was worth paying the bill for the kids to have entertainment. I did, however, find a lower-cost cable service. We don't really watch a lot of television, but when we do, the basic channels were just not enough. If you can find other options, you don't have to give up all the extras in your life. Just find a way to make it work how you can.

Be strong! Keep to your budget. Don't go on a shopping spree because you are upset or have extra money this month. Stick to your goal. Get everything paid off before you make large purchases. This is your strength in finding what you can do. Feel the accomplishment. Put a little in savings every payday. Even it is only ten dollars, every bit you invest in your future counts. Leave the savings as untouchable. Watch it grow. It will start to add up and you will feel great when you have money or when you need it for an emergency. And no, that television on sale is not an emergency.

This sense of control can be found in every situation, whether it be money, a meeting, a relationship, or even just a bad day. You do have some choice in what will happen. You have control in how you will respond. The choices you make lead you on a path. Do you want to go back down the hill and start all over? Or do you want to keep climbing to the top? Some choices will be easy, some will be hard, and each one counts.

Stress is a part of our world. Some things in this world we have no control over. We can only control our actions to what is happening around us. We cannot get out of stress, but we can control our response. These situations help define you and your character. Did you read the quote at the beginning of the chapter? You are the answer to your problems. Don't be lost during these times. Find your way. Find who you are and who you want to be. Your choices can be good or bad. Choose the good ones. You will know what they are. We all have a little voice that tells us what the good and bad is. Listen to the voice.

I have been in a life of stress. I looked at it as bad for many years. What a waste of time! I still have stress, both good and bad. I may not always make the right decisions, but I make the best ones I can. I see stress differently now.

I have a few worriers in my family. I inherited that gene, which is such a burden, but I'm finally figuring it out. I used to stress, worry, and become sick, drained, and frightened. Stress can still take a toll on me. I am human and my body will react how it does. But my mind, I can control. I have learned to face stress and learn from it. I look the situations head on and fight my way through. I control any situation I can. This is not easy. It isn't always happy, but I do it. I try to keep a positive outlook, and if things don't go how I plan, then I change the plan. I have gotten through many situations and will have many more. I know I am strong enough to handle them and will always be a fighter. The tough times help make us find who we are. Don't feel lost; find direction instead. Don't blame, don't hurt others, and don't lose control. Don't let stressful situations define who you are by letting them take you over, let how you come through define you. We will always have stress in our lives and we need to learn how to deal with it. If you made some poor choices in the past, it doesn't mean you have to make them in the future. Find who you are in the choices you make from here on out. Set a plan. Stick to it.

Follow it to the end, even though you may need to change it along the way. It is your direction, your map. Not one thing can keep you from your destination but you.

Everyone's stress is different. Some may not like giving presentations. Others may wonder why on earth someone would be so stressed about that. We are different and have different beliefs. That is OK. Just go in your direction and do not worry about anyone else but you.

I am terrified to fly. Some people enjoy it and find it safer than a car. My husband is in the Navy and he had been away for a couple years. When we married we didn't have a honeymoon. He later planned for us to meet in Hawaii for a vacation/honeymoon. I was so excited but stressed to no end. Twenty years ago I flew and I was sick for a month from the stress of it. This time I did better. I was using my mind to get me through it. Yes, I got some anxiety. Yes, I was a little sick to my stomach a few times. But I did better than I did before. I am so afraid of flying I almost did not go through with it. A few times I considered backing out. Then I asked myself, "Will I regret it if I don't do it?" The answer to this was yes. I really wanted to see my newly married man, and I had never been to Hawaii.

When I got to the TSA screening area, I just cried. I didn't want to go. I couldn't do it. Then I would think of what I would miss and not seeing my husband. I managed to get on that plane. We didn't crash, and we had a great time. I was nervous later when I knew I had to get on another plane to come home, but I managed that one, too. I now have a wonderful memory of a wonderful time. Stress comes in many different ways. Sometimes you just have to face it. The feeling of accomplishment I have is so much more amazing than if I would have let that stress and fear take over and decide not to go.

Control your actions during stressful times. Control what you can and make your direction. Even good stress can take a toll on you, having you second-guessing decisions you made, feeling overwhelmed with change, or just so excited you cannot concentrate. You can take control of the situation by making lists, planning, and focusing on the excitement instead of the stressful parts of the changes.

Learn to breathe. Relax. Take time for you. Live for the moment and think about what you can do, not what you can't. Strive to push through your stressful situations with strength and make decisions along the way. Be responsible for the choices you make.

You are what you accomplish. Even if things don't always go how you want them to, if you face things, if you try, you are still finding you, who you are, and who you want to be. Keep moving in a positive direction.

Chapter Five

Getting Positive

Things aren't really so bad

When you see it in a different way

Looking at the brighter side

This is a perfect day.

Lessons learned and choices made

To make a life I choose

I have so much I want to achieve

I have no time to lose.

When you start from the inside, it will form its way to the outside. ~td

When people feel lost, they usually also feel down or depressed. It can be a scary feeling and there is often a lot of uncertainty and lack of control. Since we have discussed some ways to gain some kind of control over different situations, now you need to get positive. Just because you are in a tough situation doesn't mean you can't be positive. In fact, you *should* be positive! Positive about the new adventures that have happened and will be happening in your life. Positive that you learned so many new things about yourself, whether good or bad. Positive that you are on your way to new discoveries, including the new you.

Even if something happens that is not so positive, you can make it a positive in your life. We change with every event in our life, whether we think we do or not. Everything puts some kind of staple in your memory and you would probably not respond the same way twice. If these events had not happened, you wouldn't be who you are today. With more events to come, you won't be the same in the future. This is good. Be positive with everything that comes your way. This is difficult. Not all things are something to be positive about, but you can learn how to keep a positive outlook.

We spend too much time thinking about the negative. Tests have even proven that the human mind will remember negative events more than it will positive ones. We think about why we hurt. How we got to where we are. Why we are not where we want to be. Well, now it is time to look at what *will* happen and be excited about the new course you are taking. Take what you learned from being hurt or mistakes you made and know how strong you are for getting through the tough stuff. Be glad about where you are right now. You are learning so much about yourself and finding out who you are. We can see the bad in everything or we can see the good. This is one of those choices you will make. Feel doomed or be happy. You are on the right path to personal success. Remember, success is not about how much money or toys you have. Success is succeeding in anything you do. Whether you reached the goal or you didn't, if you tried your best then you succeeded. Learn from mistakes. Take a new route in life. Be happy! These are choices you make.

I am going to give a few examples. A person I know just wants to be successful in his career. That was success to him. He always wanted that goal of making over $100,000 a year. He made it. He is very high in management. He is divorced, but unfortunately, most people I know are. He has a nice home, an educated daughter, lives in a great community, and so much more. The problem: he doesn't have real happiness in life and doesn't allow it to come in. He would like a woman in his life but cannot seem to find happiness with one since he is afraid of rejection. He is afraid to commit, afraid of being hurt. This has brought on a life as a workaholic, plus medical issues and unhappiness. Instead of appreciating what he has, he looks at what he doesn't have. He doesn't have a committed relationship. He doesn't have a solid structure of security in his own mind and his health is taking a toll from work and stress.

This person does go out with friends and has dates. He plays golf and is active with his community, but he does so more for acknowledgement rather than enjoyment. People adore him and give him much credit. This makes him feel good but is not fulfilling. He is down most of the time and down on life. He did have a medical scare that gave him a different outlook on some of these issues.

But you, meanwhile, should not wait until you have a medical scare to find a new outlook. A lot of people would love to be this man. In their mind, he has the ideal life. A high- salary job, community acknowledgement, and most-eligible bachelor status. So why is he not happy? It all comes down to choice.

I once talked to a woman who lost her home during the economic crisis. Many people in this situation are angry, bitter, and struggling emotionally to get through this time. Some are lost in the world and unsure of their future. This woman, however, was optimistic and positive. She was upbeat and happy. We discussed her situation and she was sad about losing her home as her family had lived there many years, and they had just finished remodeling the house. They would have been able to make the payments if the bank would've worked with them on the past due amount, but the bank refused and told them to leave their home. And they left. They are now renting a place to live from someone else.

I have heard many such stories, but this woman was different. She wasn't wallowing in self-pity, crying, whining, or being angry. I asked her how she could be so positive after everything that has happened. She said that she wasn't happy with the situation, but there was nothing they could do. They tried all of their resources, and the outcome was what it was. They were on a new adventure and looking forward to what was ahead. They are going to make the best of the situation, and even though they had to find a new place to live, their family is still together to make a new start. I told her how inspirational she was and that I admired her outlook. She said she knew everything was going to be OK and she looked forward to the future. Here is a person others would not want to be, but after losing so much in her life, she was more fulfilled than a person who seems to have it all.

Which person in these two cases would you like to be? The person who is lost in life and unhappy but seems to have everything, or the person who lost most of everything but is enjoying life? You would think the person who lost most everything would be the one who was lost, unhappy, and depressed.

It is all about the attitude. What do you possess inside yourself? Negative thoughts and a negative outlook or positive thoughts and a positive outlook? If you tend to look more toward the negative, this would be a good time to change that.

A few years ago, a woman was killed by her husband, a chief on the police force. They were going through a divorce, and they had a history of domestic violence. One day, he asked to meet her. They met in a public parking lot. On this day he pulled a gun on his wife, then shot and killed her. He then took his own life. Two young children lost both their parents that day. It was a very traumatic situation and left questions and broken hearts. Out of this tragic situation, this woman's parents and the local government made a safe zone for victims of domestic violence. It is sad that a person died in order for this to happen, but on the positive side, her parents have saved many lives. Taking a negative situation and turning it into a positive is a great way to live life. There is always a positive. You just need to find it.

Positive: having a real position, existence, or energy. Not dependent on changing circumstances or relations; opposed to negative. (Webster)

Negative: marked by denial, prohibition, or refusal; marked by absence, withholding or removal of something positive. (Webster)

Have you seen the news when a natural disaster has occurred and they interview survivors? You will see one person crying about the home they lost, their material possessions gone forever, thinking this is the most horrible thing in the world. And it is. But then you will also see a person who is so thankful that everyone is safe and thanking the Lord that they survived. They are happy and positive that they will get a new home and a new future and are just happy to have survived that experience. Two different people in the same situation but two different outlooks, one negative and the other positive. Yes, when a horrible situation takes place, we are sad, and it is OK to feel that way. The difference: the positive person knows there is something better in store for them and sees ahead. You need to see it, too.

One day, I was driving down the road with my two daughters and my daughter's friend. I was thinking about buying a new hose to wash my car since my dogs had chewed the old hose, or maybe I would go through the car wash and buy a hose later. I took a road I rarely drive, and I still don't know why I chose that route. While coming down the road on this cloudy and drizzly day, I saw a car wash fundraiser. The sign said it was for a memorial for a sixteen-year-old son killed in a hit and run. I did a quick turn around and got my car washed. Strange how I'd thought about this earlier, and then I went on a route that took me to this carwash. The people washing the cars ranged from about seven years old to about sixty years old. My heart was so sad for them. The thought of losing a child who was the age of my children who were with me that day hurt my heart. They seemed to be in very good spirits and were doing a good job on the cars. When I gave them my donation, I was taken aback by the sincere honesty they expressed when thanking me. It was an average ten dollar donation, nothing large, but they were very thankful, and you could see it in their eyes. They didn't seem to care that it was cold outside and they were working so hard with a messy, wet job. They were focused on the donations and how grateful they were to the people who pulled in for a car wash and helped them. It really stuck with me for a while, the eyes of gratitude from, I believe, the passing boy's grandmother. Grateful, positive. . . and in a horrible situation.

This life is a short one. As we grow older with every year, we see how fast the time goes. Days turn into months and months turn into years without you even noticing. Then one day you look back and notice the time is gone. Do you want to live your life in a struggle with yourself and not know where you are in life or what you're doing? Or do want to be happy and fulfilled with each day and appreciate every moment? You should enjoy every moment that you get to take a breath. One day you will not have any to take. So, enjoy. Be fulfilled. Be positive!

Life is hard on its own. Things change all the time. There are many things we have no control over. We are born, we live, and then we will pass. What we do during our time is to make a life. You are the only one who has control over that. You may not have control over what is happening, but you have choices on how you will respond. Your positive attitude will let you enjoy the life you have and let you live it to its fullest, or your negative attitude will let you float through without fulfillment and joy until one day you wonder where that time went, and now it is too late.

Right now is not too late. Right now you have a choice to change your thinking and your attitude. You have the choice to make changes you may have been putting off. You can choose to work on goals you have set aside. Right now it is up to you. It may be too late for some things, but it's not too late to change your action or direction. For instance, if you wanted to be an Olympic gymnast and you are forty years old, well, that is too late. Instead, you could start yoga, join a dance class and swing yourself around, go swimming, or start training for a marathon. You could possibly be an Olympic trainer. There are many options. There are many things I wish I would have done, but instead of going back, I am going forward and doing what I can now. Enjoy what you can at this time.

Life makes choices for you more times than not. It is up to you what you do with those choices made for you. I had a friend once tell me… "It is not what happens to you that matters, it is how you respond to what has happened that matters." I have since heard this similar quote many times. I have remembered those words and remind myself of them in situations when I am being challenged. It also helps to remind myself of those words in daily life situations. Your response defines who you are. If it is a bad situation, are you going to be all upset? Will you yell and scream? Blame others and dwell on what has happened? Or are you going to look at how this can be a positive experience and how it can make you and the future better? Sometimes it may take a while. You have to get through the experience first to see what you learned. At that time, you can determine the positive angle and turn it to a better future for you. It could be as simple as doing something different the next time or as hard as finding inner strength to get you through until the next change takes place to get you out of where you are.

I was married for twelve years. I was a wife, mother, and the homemaker for my family. I enjoyed it, loved it, and it was my life. I was happy. I didn't have to go out and socialize in dance clubs and bars in my twenties. After getting a divorce, I know I will never see my fifty-year wedding anniversary, and it is something I have always wanted. I now don't bake like I used to, and I don't have time for hobbies I started many years ago since I was raising three kids on my own. I was on the run, driving from practices to games. School programs and football games. Dances and girls going out. My son also put me through a rough couple years, and trying to handle him while keeping the girls on regular activities was hard. All the while I was working full time and caring for a home, animals, and a large yard, and wondering, *What am I doing?*

Although this is not what I have chosen for my life and didn't think it would turn out this way, I am very happy for it all. During the last ten years, I have become much stronger as a person emotionally due to the trials I have been through. Yes, it was very tough going through the trials, but I have learned so much about me that I appreciate it.

I had a sheltered upbringing and never lived on my own. I was married young and had lived with my parents until I married. I always had someone to depend on. To take care of me. To shelter me. I now had to learn to depend on myself. I needed to make the tough decisions. I needed to figure things out on my own. I needed to face things on my own. I needed to learn how to fix what is broken. I needed to be strong for my children and get them through adolescence while acting like I knew what I was doing.

I am grateful for that time I had being a single parent. Back then, I did not know that I was teaching my girls that you do not need someone to take care of you. (Well, they may be a little too independent now, but we can work on that.) I have taught my three children to be strong in times of trial. I have taught them so well that they do not ask for help and have learned to solve problems themselves. Unfortunately for me as a mom, I would like them to come to me for help, but at the same time they are strong and manage quite well. My son is a wonderful man. He worked through his teenage experiences, and they have made him a better person. While some of his friends are not growing up well, he is working and providing for his family. His experience taught him, as well as me and his sisters, that we can overcome and pull through rough situations.

Take the positive of what is handed to you. Learn from the experiences. Trials make you strong. Are they tough? Yes. Otherwise it wouldn't be a trial. Is a jury in your mind waiting to find you guilty of being a negative person, or will it find you to be a positive person learning from your trials? You can find the strength to overcome. Bad things happen in this world every day, every minute, and every second. We can wish the bad stuff away, but in reality, bad stuff is everywhere. You cannot hide from it. Eventually it will find you. All that you can do is find your strength to get through.

Have you known a person who is dying but is nonetheless happy and still saying positive things to those around them? You may wonder how on earth this person can be so happy when they are going to die. In reality, we are all going to die. The only difference is this person knows when. When you live a full life (not measured by years), you can accept the bad stuff more easily than if you are a negative person. The fulfilled person may be scared and sad about leaving this earth, sick from illness or in pain....but they know they have lived, and they're ready to take in the final chapter of their life on earth. Death is very hard to accept, but there is positive for some in these cases, too. If they have been very ill, the suffering and pain will be over for them when they cross over. In their final days, they can teach valuable lessons and maybe even save someone else if they are an organ donor.

People who are positive to the end inspire us. We remember them being so full of life and we only hope we can be a little of what they taught us. These are the people who leave marks on our hearts. Remember, we can all leave marks on hearts, while we're alive or when we're passing. Whenever positive energy is handed to someone else, it stays. The feeling it leaves behind is special.

Even if you are having a bad day, someone else may be, too. We don't need to be negative and upset. Open the door for someone. Pick up something that has been dropped. Check on an elderly neighbor. If you have the funds, leave a larger tip. When you help make someone's day, it also makes your day better. Don't pass forward the negative; instead spread the positive. It doesn't mean to put all your feelings aside; it just means that when we are having a tough time, we don't have to make it tough for others, too. If they had nothing to do with your bad time, why give them negative energy? And even if you are having a bad time, someone may be going through something even worse. And a little positive energy passed on can make a huge difference. You may never know the positive impact you have on another person.

Keep up the positive thoughts, actions, and emotions. Do not let negative overtake you and keep you down. You will feel better about you and about life. One positive action leads to another, and what comes around, goes around. Keep it going around in a positive light!

Chapter Six

Let it Go

Put the past behind

Move on to the new

Find a great adventure

There are no limits for you.

The past holds you back

There is so much more in store

Cut the strings that hold you down

Go out and explore!

If you lost the key to your baggage, you have been carrying it for too long.

~td

Pain, the hurt we feel from others and ourselves, is inevitable. However, if you keep painful thoughts in your mind often and you can't seem to move forward because the past is holding you back, LET IT GO! These thoughts can stop you from enjoying your future.

We have all experienced some pain in our lives and we will experience more in the future. It is a part of life we would like to avoid but still remains to be there. How you choose to deal with pain is completely up to you. You can dwell on it and let it hold you back from living a fulfilling life, or you can put it behind you and move on strong and free. The harder choice is to move on. Remember, moving forward does not mean forgetting what has happened; it means you are choosing to not be held back by it.

You may be someone (or know someone) who has had something bad or tragic happen in their life and the words, "I just can't let it go!" come out. We *can* let it go, but sometimes we choose to hold on. Sometimes we cling out of comfort because once we let it go, there is a void, an absence. We are not sure what to do. It may seem strange, but that burden is a comfort at the same time it is pulling us down. It is easier to keep it in our life than to let it go and move on. But once you take the steps to start releasing it, the easier it will be.

Relationships are a good example. If you have been hurt or cheated on and your walls are built up, it is easier to keep ruining future relationships rather than to be happy. Sound strange? It is, but it happens. If you don't let anyone come totally in, then you are protecting yourself. If you don't become complete with a new relationship, then it will not hurt as much if it ends. You are always preparing yourself for that end, and your guard is up to protect your heart when it is over. At the same time you probably say, "Relationships never last. I am tired of trying. I am tired of being hurt." What you are really saying is what I fear, I will manifest. When you look at the situation, are you really trying? Do you compare new relationships to the past ones? If you were cheated on, do you suspect your new partners to be cheaters too? If you were treated poorly before and the new person is nice, are you suspecting it can't be real and there is something wrong? Are they too nice and it scares you?

We are all a little wary when meeting someone new. We fear pain or loss. But why do we continue to hurt ourselves when we want love and happiness? We are not going to find a loving relationship if we don't give it a chance. Each new person is exactly that: a new person, a new personality, a new chance, and new excitement. Remember what we said before: if a relationship doesn't work, learn from it. Some relationships are just learning experiences to take you to the next one. Go into the new relationship open minded. It could be the best thing ever or a learning tool. To treat a person poorly in fear of being hurt is not fair to the person or you. That usually does not allow for a happy ending. This is not the person who hurt you, so don't treat them that way. You don't have to open your heart right away, but at least give it a chance and enjoy your time and experience.

It can be anything holding you back: the passing of a loved one, the loss of a job, low self-esteem, being insecure in life, or just about anything that you have no control over. People forget that the past is just the past. It is not today and it won't be tomorrow. It is past, behind you and to be left there. You should feel excited about what is next, not dwell on what has been left behind. This does not mean it has not changed your life. It has brought you to where you are today and where you will go in the days ahead.

There may be things that will be with you the rest of your life. Things that you cannot easily *let go* but can move forward from. I know a few women who have been sexually assaulted. This is something you cannot just *let go*. It does not, however, mean you cannot move forward and find strength to have a happy, loving relationship, or a much better life. Many of these women deal with guilt and shame, and in some cases feel like the suspect, not the victim. They feel like the crime was their fault. If they had not been drinking. If they had not worn those kind of clothes. If they had not been jogging in the woods. If they weren't out after dark. So many ifs. This would be enough to take a large toll on any person. You need to get through it day by day and seek counseling in many cases. But even something as tragic as this can make you a much stronger person. You can come through it with pride of being who you are and strength to master the days ahead.

Many men are now coming out and discussing their assaults. There are many women and men who are now consultants and speakers using a horrible situation to help others. They don't let their painful experience bring them down in life, and they have found the courage to use it as a tool to help others. This does not happen overnight, but every step you take will make letting go easier. This is true with many situations that can weigh you down.

You need to acknowledge what burden you carry. Why have you not let go? What is holding you back? The most common answer is fear. Fear of the unknown. Fear that when you let it go, you are saying you no longer care. Fear of guilt.

If someone we love passes away, we mourn. We have our grieving time and at some point we move on. Some people have a hard time moving on out of the guilt around being happy. What gives them the right to be happy? Losing a loved one is one of the hardest things to live with. That hurt is the greatest hurt there is to the heart.

We are all eventually going to move on from this life. You must live now, while you are still here. It is not bad to be happy in life. It is not bad to laugh and have good times when someone else has passed. Their time in life is over and it may have been short or very long, but they will not be coming back. If you are given the opportunity to continue living on earth, you need to use this time to live. Do not feel shame when happy moments come your way. There is a time to move forward and enjoy the world again. We don't ever stop missing, loving, and remembering the person we lost, but we can keep moving forward with our own lives and should not feel guilt in doing so. Let the pain and sadness go. Move on and be happy.

Many times we put our burdens on ourselves. No one handed them to us—we took them willingly. You don't need to carry them any longer. The burden of what is weighing you down or holding you back can be taken off and dropped off at the next corner. Then leave it there and keep on going. Just keep moving further and further away from it until it is not in sight. Do not carry it into your future. Make room in your life for a new adventure and keep heading in the direction you want to be moving in.

Many family members carry grudges. A little thing like a family disagreement at a holiday dinner makes some people hold a grudge for years, not speaking to each other. What is the grudge doing to other family members? It is not just the people with the grudges that are involved. Some gatherings aren't held due to the awkwardness it may cause. Some people won't show up if people holding the grudge are invited. People have to watch what they say so they won't seem to be taking sides or hurting someone's feelings if they spoke to the person another person is still angry with. It becomes a problem for many people over something that could have been let go. Now the "grudgers" can't move on, and others around them can't either.

To let go of something may feel like you're showing weakness. If you "give in" then you are not strong. But letting go is not weakness. Keeping the burden and holding onto the past is easier than letting it go and apologizing. Strength is not always about how tough you think you are. When we carry hurt, disappointment, or pain, we may not be the only one who has to carry it. It gets passed to others as well. We are not here to live in the past; we are here to live in the present and move on to the future. There is so much ahead of us to go out and live for. You can't do that if you keep looking in the rearview mirror and holding these thoughts with you.

Do you still have your list of values? Go find the list and take a look at it. Are you living the way you want to live? Are you putting these values in your life? Is there something holding you back from moving forward and living the way you want? Then let it go. This is where you will find another piece of you. This is where you will see what you have inside to move one step further in the right direction. This book is about finding you. Finding the direction you want to go. You cannot move in the right direction if you keep holding on to the past. The past is a learning experience in life to take you on your next step.

One way to let go is to stop asking questions. *Why did this happen to me? Why did that person have to pass away? Why didn't I get the promotion? Why can't I be rich and stop struggling every day? Why, why, why?* Many of these questions will not be answered, and trying to figure them out is holding you back from moving ahead.

There are plenty of things in this world I could be dwelling on. A failed marriage, missed promotions, bad dating experiences, mental and physical abusive relationships, and so much more. But what good is it to sit and sulk? Stewing uses so much of your energy and drains you emotionally and physically. Who wants to be tired or emotionally drained every day over something you cannot change? Whatever happened has happened. It is over and done. You can't change the past. But you can use it towards a better future.

Interestingly, when you do let things go, people close to you may have something to say about it. If you have been burdened and are now moving on toward a better life, some may not accept it. Do not let that bother you. Keep on moving. Some people thrive on watching others suffer, mostly because they are suffering themselves in some way and don't have the strength to move forward. These people may be angry or jealous if they see you moving on with your life in a positive way. Do not let this set you back. Whatever issue someone has with you is their issue. It is not yours. Do not feel guilty, do not feel bad, and do not let them bring you back. Keep putting one step in front of the other.

Being a parent is a very hard job. We want to do what is right for our children. In many families, the children come first. As a single mom, I struggled to make ends meet so my kids could still do the sports they loved, wear fashionable (not expensive) clothes at school to fit in, and have presents under the tree every year at Christmas. I dated during this time, but my children were always first and I never missed a sports game. (Well, I missed one when I had a class, but I never did that again, because of course, my daughter fell at that game and was injured.)

Anyway, my life is my children. When I unexpectedly fell in love and my boyfriend (now husband) received orders to be sent to Guam, after turning down the invitation to move to Guam, I offered to rent my home and move forty-five minutes away to care for his mini-farm while he was gone. I had one child left in school, a junior in high school. The guilt I had over this was horrible. What on earth was I thinking? I'd always put my kids first, and now I was moving my daughter in a precious year of high school, possibly ruining her!

For two years I suffered with this decision I made. I felt like I'd let my kids down. I was messing up their lives. With only one left in school and the other two in young adulthood, I was still thinking of them as elementary children who needed much protection. This single mom thought I was all they needed, that I was the key to their happiness. Even though they agreed with the move and said it was now my turn to live for me, I still felt bad. I finally had to let this go. I had been hanging on to it for too long. The move had been made, we were living at the farm, and I couldn't go back and change what I did. Yes, I could move back to my home, but that wouldn't change what had already happened. Adjustments in life had already been made.

This is an example of a burden I put on myself. No one gave it to me—I took it. It was my guilt as a mom thinking I may have let my kids down. I wasn't focusing only on them, and I made a decision based on a man. Moving my children because of a man. I let someone else in our family and made a decision based on him. Being an adult, I have a right to do this. I was not putting my kids in harm's way. I was not neglecting my children. I included them and their thoughts in the decision. Yet I placed a burden on myself out of guilt.

As a result, I was not allowing myself to be fully happy. I am a happy person generally, but I was not fully happy in my living situation. I was not accepting this place as my home. It was not my family's home. It could never be the home my kids could come back to years later. But many people move when their kids graduate from school. Where I grew up, most all of my friends' parents have moved from the area. I just wasn't raised that way, though. My parents still live in the house I was raised in from the time I was nine. Although my children will not have the same experience, they are doing well and two of my children are still living at the farm.

Releasing this kind of burden gives you a physical lift as the weight comes off your shoulders. Many times you can actually feel the difference when the burden has lifted.

My living situation is an example of how it doesn't even have to be a very painful or tragic situation to let something keep you from moving on. A burden can be anything your mind allows. I let go of the hurt of a failed marriage, the low self-esteem of mental abuse, and the loss of dear ones no longer here. I was upset when I got passed for promotions and let it stew for a bit. Then it needed to go. I'm enjoying moving forward and seeing what life brings. My direction may have changed a few times, but I like my direction today.

I know a woman who constantly dwells on the past. She holds on to things, staying in drama because she stays in a holding pattern with all the hurt and pain. This life has also led her to be an alcoholic because the pain is too much to bear, but she will not let it go and move forward. Her life is not fulfilling and she does not like it. She is depressed and unhappy with most things.

Sometimes it is harder to be happy than to be sad. Discontent can become our comfort zone. If you have burdened yourself for so long, life without the burdens is scary. To be free is not normal that way. To have energy and a life of adventure may not be expected. But I want to tell you it is how you were meant to live. Living the life of LIFE is what you should be doing. You were not meant to stay in the past and hold yourself back. You were meant to make a difference in everything you do and fulfill your life with good things that you enjoy and that make you happy.

This is a decision. This is a life you will have to choose. This is your journey to finding you and your direction in life. Once you pass the stop sign and start moving forward, there is a new world for you to explore. It is waiting for you.

Take small steps to let go of the past, one foot forward at a time. One day you will look back and see how far you have come. Then when you look back, it won't be to dwell on your past. You will be looking at what you left behind.

Chapter Seven

Loving You

I am the only one like this

No other can compare

I love me for who I am

Not for an image or clothes I wear.

When I look in the mirror

I like the reflection I see

Because there is no one else

Who is molded just like me.

The reflection you see about yourself begins by not looking in a mirror.

~td

If you have been in a lost state of mind, then chances are you are not feeling too good about yourself. Usually when people are heading the direction they want to be going, they love who they are. When you are uncertain of yourself and your potential, you can feel lost. But even the most confident people don't have all the answers to their purpose in life. They just follow the direction that life takes them on, and they enjoy the ride.

You are the most important person in your life. You will be stuck with you for your entire life, longer than you'll be with anyone else on this planet. You can't walk away from yourself. You can't block yourself. You can't delete yourself as a friend. You are stuck with you wherever you go. So you might as well enjoy the person who is you. Sure, you may have made some bad decisions. You have been hurt by people. You have struggled through things no one else will understand the way you do. You may not be the weight you want to be. You may not have the job you want. You may not live in house you dreamed of. You may not be where you wanted to be at this point in your life. There could be many reasons you may look at yourself unhappily, but you are still you. You are where you are today because of being you. You made decisions to get yourself to this day. You also have choices and decisions to get yourself where you will be tomorrow or five years from now.

Just because things have not gone well for you in some situations does not mean you need to be down on yourself. Love who you are. We are all individually made to serve differently in the world. Not everyone will appreciate what you have to offer, but some will be very grateful. We cannot please everyone that we come across no matter how hard we try. We can only please ourselves and know that what we are offering is original and given with good intent.

In the previous chapter, I mentioned that I was mentally abused. Words were said to me that made me feel unworthy as a mother, a provider, or a human being. I remember that by the time I was going through my divorce, I had felt that dirt was a precious item compared to me. I am not exaggerating when I say I actually felt that dirt had more worth than my existence. It has taken many years for me to feel OK about myself. I have let go of the pain, but I will not forget how it made me feel, and some things remain with me. Just because you still may carry some baggage, doesn't mean you cannot appreciate yourself for who you are. Baggage does not take away your greatness. And someday all the baggage will be left behind.

Looking back, I see that what was said to me was not true, but when you are living in the situation, you tend to believe it. If you are in a situation such as this, do not let negative words take away your value. Do not let those words soak into your belief system. You are a good person. You may have done some things that you are not proud of, but that does not make you a bad person. There is room in your future for more decisions, and one of them is liking who you are.

If you want to change your path, change how you feel about yourself. Look in the mirror every day and say one good thing about yourself. It can be as simple as, "I have nice fingers. They are not too long or too short, but just right." Every day acknowledge something good about you. Are you a hard worker? Do you meet deadlines? Are you always on time? Are you a good planner? Are you artistic? Do you have a beautiful voice? Are you good with numbers? There are many good qualities that you possess, and you need to appreciate them. Focus on your good and not your bad.

Are you down and out because you are overweight? Do you feel ugly? Do you feel unworthy since you don't look like the model-thin people we view in magazines and ads? Don't do that to yourself. There is one particular movie star who is the same age as I am and I look *nothing* like her. She is very beautiful, no wrinkles, flat stomach. It makes me wonder why I don't look like that at the same age. For one thing, she has had no children; I have three. She has a personal trainer; I have a home gym. She has stylists and buys expensive facial products. I have a flat iron in my bathroom and I buy products I see on TV.

Do not compare yourself to other people. It is very unrealistic. We are all different in our own ways. While I long for her looks, she longs for a family, which she has never had. I have been blessed with three wonderful children while she yearns to be a mother. I have a private life that is not scattered all over the tabloids while she has to conceal herself to go out in public. Do not compare your life. Be happy and accept the one you have.

One thing that does make me feel good about myself is exercise. I feel better after a workout and I like that I am doing something for only me. It is work but it is worth it. Anything worthwhile involves work. If you are not happy with the way you look, do you exercise? Talk to your doctor and see if it is safe for you before you start any kind of exercise program. If you get approval, try small things to get started. Maybe take a walk for fifteen minutes to get the body moving. Slowly work your way to longer walk times. Add a few minutes every other week. It may not feel fun at first and it may be a stress to you, but if you continue with it, you will get stronger and it will become more enjoyable. I am not a skinny model-type girl. Never have been. I exercise because it makes me feel good. When I see changes in my body, it boosts my confidence even more.

There may be things you won't even notice about yourself until one day something surprises you. For example, I have always had a burning thigh problem. Even in school, I remember my thighs would burn when I did certain moves in gym class. It was hard to walk up stairs or hills because my thighs would hurt. One day my husband and I climbed a hill in Hawaii. At the top, we could either walk up a trail or climb an enormous number of stairs. I chose the stairs. Why not? I had been working out for a few months, but not on vacation. (It was vacation—why should I?) Expecting to stop a few times up the stairs, I was astonished when we came to the top and I had not stopped even once to rest or recover from burning thighs. That to me was more exciting than losing five pounds. My body was getting stronger. You can't see that in a mirror necessarily, but you can feel it. Remember to appreciate these small accomplishments when you notice them.

Before I went on this trip to Hawaii, I had to deal with my fear of flying. It had been almost twenty years since the last time I had flown. I had been afraid even back then, too. This time, I had almost cancelled, but my husband was waiting for me on the other side of that airplane ride. Since he was stationed in Guam and we'd recently married, we planned to meet in Hawaii for a little postponed honeymoon. I was going to fly alone. Over water. In a plane. By myself. I was terrified.

I actually cried in fear when I got to the TSA station. They just let me go by, and I am sure they just didn't want to deal with a freaked-out passenger. I kept asking myself the question, "Would I regret it if I don't go?" The answer was yes, because I missed my husband, I had never been to Hawaii, and I wanted to experience something new. I got on the plane, apologized to the people seated next to me for having to sit by me, and we took off.

I did have fear, but I just thought that if it was my time to go, then it would be my time. If not, then I would land and then have a great time. I am still here, so I landed and had a great time. Of course I dealt with the fear again having to come home, but I made that trip too. I cannot tell you how proud of myself I was. Facing a fear is very difficult, but to accomplish it will bring you a moment of such joy. It also made me proud to be me. The person I am stuck with for the rest of my life had a wonderful time with no regrets, moving one step closer to a direction I wanted to take myself.

What do you want to accomplish? Have you taken steps to move in the direction you want to go? When you start appreciating who you are, your confidence takes you in directions you couldn't even imagine. Take it one step at a time. Make choices that please you. This is your life and you are the only one living it to the end. You need to do things that please you and make you feel good about who you are. Loving yourself is not being conceited or selfish. Loving yourself is enjoying you for who you are.

Some people seem to love themselves a little too much. Everything is always about them. Life revolves around them. That is not what I am talking about. I am talking about feeling good about who you are. There is nothing better in life than loving who you are and sharing yourself with good people around you.

Some people are very beautiful, but they have a low self-esteem. They hound themselves every day about not looking good enough, not being thin enough, not being better than what they are. They are unsure of what they are doing in the world, trying to please everyone else and only making themselves sad in the meantime. Outside beauty has nothing to do with feeling confident and loving who you are. Your beauty comes from the inside. Loving yourself comes from the inside. It is not what the eyes see—it is how you feel. When you feel good about who you are, it will show on the outside.

In my last job, I was passed over for a promotion twice. It was pretty heart-wrenching. The person who got the promotion was not a team player. My other co-workers had constant complaints about this person, and she was a complainer herself. She was also very controlling and did not follow standard procedures; she did what she wanted to do. The other employees and I followed procedures and always tried to work as a team. After the decision was made that this person would be our lead worker, it was devastating to many of us. It seemed very unfair, and many people were hurt. It felt like the ones who worked hard at being a team were not appreciated for doing what they thought they should be doing. I personally knew I could do well at that job.

Then feeling not good enough came into play. Maybe I am not as good as I thought. Maybe I am not a good employee. Maybe I don't know my job like I thought I did. Why wasn't I chosen? What is wrong with me? Then I sank a little bit inside myself and questioned my abilities as a person. Anger set in. Angry because when you thought you were doing everything you were supposed to be doing, someone got the lead worker job who wasn't even a team player.

This struggle would also fall under the Let it Go chapter. You can't hold on to the anger. You have to let it go. It is something you cannot change, and it is a learning experience.

I finally asked one of the reviewers on the panel why this person was chosen. She said that good or bad, she always made suggestions on different ways to do jobs. She thought outside of the box, and that is what they wanted for the position. Although it made sense, it still didn't take away all the pain. I had decided that it wasn't meant to be, and I would still do a very good job at what I do and not let the decision affect my work. I knew I was good at what I did but it wasn't meant for me to have the promotion. I let it go. Shortly after that, I was moved to a new position. It was not a promotion, but it took me to a job I really enjoyed. I did very well at the new position. I really liked the new coworkers and there was not nearly as much stress at the new job. Looking back, although it hurt my ego not to get a promotion, if I'd gotten it, I would have been in a very stressful job and not feeling as fulfilled as I did in the new position. And the person who did get the promotion, is doing a fantastic job. Honestly, she was the better choice. Sometimes the pain is more pride than the situation.

Sometimes it is not about money or a title, but instead a way of life. I'd worked in a very stressful environment for many years, and the new position was a nice change. I am a firm believer that everything happens for a reason. I was once again confident in my work abilities, and I believe that letting go leads you to better things ahead. And just because someone else is chosen, doesn't mean you are not good, it just means you weren't chosen. Something better may be waiting for you.

Even in a painful situation, I worked on keeping my confidence up. I used this time as a test of how I would respond. It was difficult and took me back a step or two, but then I kept walking forward. You are the only one who can love yourself and build yourself up. Yes, people in your life can support you and help you feel good about yourself. It is nice to hear from others how wonderful you are. But you need to be confident in yourself and love who you are. The other people are just confirming it.

Don't wait for something to happen to start loving yourself. Too many times I hear, "When I fall in love, I will feel better about myself" or "When I get such and such, I will be happy." Don't wait to start feeling happy and loving who you are based on a situation. Situations change. You are the only you, and that will not go away. Start appreciating who you are now. When you love who you are, the situations only get better. Another person doesn't make you love who you are. A situation can't guarantee happiness. This all depends on you. You are the one who makes you happy. You are the one who controls your feelings about yourself.

I know a woman who always feels unhappy unless she is in a relationship. She needs a man in order to feel happy. When she is not in a relationship, she is not confident about herself, and her attitude changes. The minute she is in a relationship, she is happy, smiling, and feeling good about herself. If that relationship ends, she is back to feeling down about herself, and her confidence hits the floor.

It is not healthy to bounce back and forth about what you feel about yourself based on being with another person. Mostly the relationships do not last because the feelings she has about herself are based on situations. Other people can see how you feel about yourself if you let them get close enough to you. Even though most men want to be the king of the relationship, they prefer a woman who possesses confidence in herself. Not too much confidence that might overpower the relationship, but enough confidence that she can stand for herself and her self-worth. The same goes for what a woman wants in a man. Not a controlling man who thinks he is boss, but a confident man who wants to have the woman at his side.

Love who you are alone. Even if you are in a relationship now, do not love who you are *because* of who you are with. Love yourself because it is the only you that you have. Love who you are because you deserve it. When you feel good about who you are, the world changes around you. You enjoy things more than you did before. You look forward to new experiences. You look forward to challenging yourself. You don't fall so hard when you fail because you try a new route and try again. You only have one life, and you were given *you* to live this life in. Enjoy what was given to you. Love who you are and the moments that come day to day with new adventures to look forward to.

There can be no better joy in finding you when you discover the love you have for yourself. Loving who you are is best way to finding who you truly are and where you want to be.

Chapter Eight

Change with the Change

Change is a part of life

There is nothing you can do

So make your changes in your world

And have an adventure or two.

If everything stayed the same

How boring that would be

Go where life takes you

Change is what sets you free.

Every moment of your day changes you in a different way. ~td

With so many changes in this world, it is bound to happen: you don't know where you are going and you've lost your sense of direction. You had it all planned, and then something happens that changes everything. You can't continue to go the direction you were going, and this wasn't in the plan. What do you do now?

It is ok. You are right where you are meant to be. Sometimes our plans are not the plans that are in store for us. At times like this, look at the bigger picture. We focus so much on how we think things should be rather than what is meant to be.

We previously discussed many situations that can make you feel lost. When you look at many of them, change is the big factor. Things change all the time, but in our minds, we like to keep things the same. Change is scary. Change is unknown. But change happens. It may take you off the path you were heading, but it doesn't mean you won't get there eventually. You just need to make a new route. The direction is the same—the path you are heading is just taking a detour. It can also be that the path you were heading was not the right one for you, and a change was needed to get you on the right path.

I see problems with co-workers when changes happen. Whenever someone is moved out of their comfort zone, it is stressful. Even if the change is for the good, it will turn into a fiasco with a few people. Very often you will hear someone say, "Why do we need to change it? It was fine the way it was." A simple change in the way of doing things turns into a complaint session and a major discussion and meetings. Some people do not adapt well to change. It causes stress, fear, and loss of control. That is what the real issue is with change: loss of control. I mentioned before that lack of control can cause a person to feel lost. It is not enjoyable to live when you have no control over your surroundings. You don't know which way to go or what will be next.

When change does come your way, you *do* have control over how you will handle it. That response is all the control you need to keep you moving in the right direction. It may be unsettling in the beginning, but when you take control over your response, you will be in the right place.

Some people find change to be the hardest thing to adjust to and others seem to go with the flow. Nothing seems to bother them and they just keep moving forward seemingly untouched. Some people are just that way, but for others it took them some practice to get there. When you understand that you cannot do anything about the change that has occurred, you will understand that how you respond will make all the difference. Take down your guard and stop fighting the change. The fight is what causes you to lose yourself and direction.

I wasn't planning on being a divorced single mom. That was not in my plan at all. I couldn't control the situation, but I could control how I handled it. At the beginning, I did not handle it well. The loss of control over what was happening in my life was overwhelming. I had to live alone and take care of three elementary-school-aged children. I had to care for a home and work full-time, living on my salary plus child support. Many changes needed to happen because of one change. It took a while for me to adjust.

To start, I kept my kids in the sports they were playing. I wanted some kind of normalcy, plus it was a good outlet for them while they were going through the changes themselves. I made sure the dogs stayed with the kids since they had grown up with them and they (the dogs) were a sense of security. I made sure the kids kept play dates and went to events. I controlled what I could and I was determined to get through it the best way I knew how. It was not easy, and even doing what I thought was best still didn't keep the kids from the pain of the divorce.

You can only do what you think is best and make choices that will help you make a new way. It may take a couple of different turns and a few hills, but eventually the road will smooth out and the ride will be easier to handle. If you fight it, the road will be bumpy. Keep turning in the wrong direction, and you will feel lost with no map to find your way.

Don't fight it. Move with the changes. Continue to change the way you think about the situation. Even though you don't like the change, think of the positive that is happening, also. I didn't like the change of the divorce itself, but I like what the change has brought to my life and to me personally. I am a much better person today.

Every day we change. We may feel that we aren't, but think about it: are you the same as you were when you were two years old? Of course not. Do you still feel the same way about certain things as you did ten years ago? Probably not. It seems that as we get older, we don't have the same mindset. We become wiser and stronger. We change without noticing it. It is only the noticeable changes that seem to affect us in a negative way. The ones we were not expecting. The ones that force us to make noticeable changes to ourselves.

Have you moved away from where you grew up, gone back to see the old stomping ground, and found that it looks completely different? The old post office is now a restaurant, and the place you used to hang out in the woods is now all built up with houses? If you were still living there when the changes were taking place, you'd have noticed, but you would adjust easily because you were watching the process. When you leave and come back to everything looking different, the change is dramatic. It doesn't feel like home.

I grew up in a small town. We moved there when I was nine. It was a very wooded area, and the main section of town was fifteen minutes away. Main street was a chuck-holed road with a tavern, a couple gas stations, a couple banks, a post office, and a tire center. Oh, and a feed store and a nursery. When I was living there, a few more stores and restaurants were built as well.

I moved away from there over twenty years ago. My parents still live in the same house I grew up in from the time I was nine years old. I normally drive the back way to my parents' house, but one day my mom wanted to go into town. I was in complete shock. They had a cinema, many restaurants, a shopping center, new stores—it looked like a completely different place than where I grew up. I didn't even recognize some of the roads I used to drive since there was so much development. It didn't feel like home anymore to me. My mom didn't think anything of it since she had watched these changes take place. It was not the same as when we moved there, but the changes were not as noticeable to her as they were for me when I saw them all at once.

That situation is the same with life. Things are changing every day, but we are flowing with most of them and we don't tend to notice. When a transition hits us that we must make changes in our own lives for, it is huge! It throws everything off course, and we have a hard time adjusting to it. We need to treat it as a gradual change that takes place every day. We need to flow with it and not let it make a negative impact.

We tend to drive the same routes over and over. The same roads, the same stop signs, and traffic lights. You can leave the house at the same time each day, but you are not driving with the same cars every day. There are some you see again and again, but mostly the other cars are different. It may feel like the same situation but the cars change on a regular basis. Do you even notice that? Not really, because you are driving on the same roads and hitting the same lights, so you feel that the situation is the same. But it isn't. Every day the people you are driving with are different. There may be a car accident one day, and you encounter unexpected traffic. A road may be closed and you have to take an alternate route. These changes are frustrating and can become stressful, but you adjust to them. You will leave earlier tomorrow to adjust your time to accommodate the detour. You may have exited sooner to avoid the car accident up ahead. Inconvenient, yes, but you changed your direction, and besides being stressed about being late to work, you probably didn't think much about it.

That is how you need to adjust to changes in life. You take a detour on your plan and make a different route. You adjust to what accidents may lay ahead and choose a different path to get by them. It may be inconvenient at first, but then it becomes routine. Maybe the new route you chose to take is better than the prior one, and you will continue to go that way instead.

Change can be good. What seemed inconvenient at the beginning turned out to the best change that could happen. This is another reason not to fight the changes in your life. The changes are putting you on the path you were meant to be taking. Sometimes a little push is needed to get you there.

A woman I know was working in retirement homes and caring for the elderly for many years. Years of this hard physical work had taken a toll on her own body. She started to develop arthritis and later found out that she had fibromyalgia. It was getting difficult for her to lift patients without pain. She was going home very sore and tired. Her family insisted that she needed to find a new job. The problems she was having with her body were affecting her job performance, and she was starting to have issues at work. She refused to take the advice of her family and seek new employment. She had done this work for over twenty years, and to find something else was too far out of her comfort zone. She would endure the pain instead of trying to find a new job that worked with her physical ailments.

Eventually the problems at work became worse, and her employer let her go. This was unexpected, and she was now unemployed. She had no choice but to find another job. With the added stress of filing for unemployment benefits and getting behind in her bills, she felt she'd lost control. The stress was creating new problems with her pain, and she was fighting this change in her life every step of the way. She wanted her job back. She was fighting the termination with her employer. She would not adjust to the change until she had no other choice but to move forward. She was forced into this change when instead she could have had control *in the beginning.*

Moving out of your comfort zone can be stressful regardless, but when you're forced out of it, it's much harder. Sometimes when we are in a place we are not meant to be, we need a push to get us out of that situation and into a new one. This woman did eventually find a new job in a different field and has made many new changes because of the situation given to her.

Sometimes we want the change, but it doesn't happen. That can be frustrating when you are trying to move forward and see road blocks ahead. For example, my daughter was working when I moved to the farm. She was trying to transfer to a job so she could move over to the farm as well. She applied many times and was not accepted. Although she was working with the same company and had experience, she was not being offered a job. It took her a year of applying before she finally got on at the

121

new location. During that year, she was very frustrated. She had a plan and it was not working out. But she did not give up. She had to adjust her plans, but she kept moving forward and did not let road blocks make her change the direction she wanted to go. If the change is meant to be, it will happen. It may take you longer, but if you do not give up, you will succeed.

When you are the one who wants the change but it is not happening yet, it is not the right time. There could be something you need to learn before making that change. There may be something better after the long wait. When we want change, we want it now! We are willing to adjust everything for the change we want. What we don't like is when the change comes to us when are not expecting it and then we need to adjust our lives around it.

In reality, though, these changes are all the same. They all need adjustments. When changes come into our lives, we need to accept them for what they are. If there is nothing we can do about what is happening, then we need to flow with the change. Why are we willing to make a change in our life whenever we want but not willing to make the adjustments when the change comes to us? Control.

Learn to control yourself within the situations you have. When my daughter was trying to transfer over to the new location, she knew it would be a big change, and she was willing to do it. She had to make adjustments when that change did not take place. There was disappointment. Many times. Then when she finally got a job offer, she was scared. She had been planning for this change for a long time, but when it finally happened it was a shock. Now she really had to move. She was leaving her comfort zone of her current employer and would be working in a new location with new co-workers. What if they did not get along? What if they did not like her? What if she didn't like the new location? Change comes with many what-ifs, and they can drive you crazy. Ignore the what-ifs when change takes place. Asking the what-ifs is the same thing as fighting the change, and this kind of thinking makes your adjustment all the more difficult.

When I moved to the farm, I asked myself many what-if questions. What if I don't like it? What if I can't take care of the animals? What if something bad happens? What if someone gets sick? I was moving out of my comfort zone. The answers would be the same as if I was staying in my own home. I would still have the same control, but since I was moving out of my comfort zone, it felt like I was losing all of my control. The mind can make things difficult or it can make things easy. Change happens every day and usually does not affect you physically. It is the mind that the change affects. Do not let negative thoughts control your mind when change occurs. Use your mind to control what you can. Use your mind to allow you to flow with the change. Use your mind to accept the change. Use your mind to allow the change to put you in the right direction.

Using your mind means discovering more about who you are. Use your mind to help set you free when change occurs and use the change as a guiding post toward the right direction in which you are to be heading. These changes would not be taking place if it is not where you were meant to be. Don't fight the change. Change with the change.

Chapter Nine

Follow Your Dreams

Dreamers of the world

Bring new hope and light

Following their dreams

With no boundaries in sight.

Hopeful to the end

Yet a new beginning seen

For the ones who never give up hope

On following their dreams.

If you never start... your dream will never become a reality. ~td

Some people say dreamers don't live in reality. I say dreamers *make* our reality. If we didn't have dreamers, we wouldn't be flying in airplanes, taking trains, driving cars, touring theme parks, enjoying music, and so much more. The dreamers who gave us those inventions made their dreams reality. Look at the all the computers we use today, thanks to the dreamers who created computer software. If they did not pursue their dream, where would we be today? It starts with a thought that turns into a dream. It is up to you to go for it—or let it pass as a moment of time that slips away.

Many amazing people had a dream for many years and never gave up. Look at how many woman try out to be football cheerleaders. Some do not make it their first time, but with determination they go back the next year and try again. Or consider the Olympians who set out to reach the dream of competing for a gold medal. There are people in their senior years of life graduating from college. Every day you can turn on your television and see sponsored programs of people selling items they invented. Dreams are not for people who do not live in reality. Dreamers create reality. You can transform your dream into reality.

I once heard from a preacher that dreams are seeds God has planted inside of you. It is up to you to make the seed grow. I believe this statement. A dream would not have come to your mind if it wasn't intended for you to act on. I've said many times how life would be so much easier if they would just make such-and-such. Then a couple years later, that such-and-such was being sold on the market. Had I taken that thought and turned it into a dream and pursued it, it would have been my invention. But I'd just passed the thought off like a moment of time. Didn't think any more about it. Someone else had the same thought. They took the same seed and made it grow. They pursued a dream and made it a reality.

When we think about why some things turn out the way they do, we look back and wonder why we didn't do something about it. We don't always acknowledge our thoughts as potentially becoming something big. They're just thoughts. Then there are times when the thought is more than just a thought, and we ponder it regularly. We dream about the dream we want to achieve. Sometimes we just don't know how to start working on that dream. Where do we begin?

Dreams are large goals. Sometimes you need to set up many goals to reach the ultimate one. You can find information online today on just about anything. Do your research and see what information you can find to assist you. Contact people who may be able to help you. Seeking help and guidance does not make your dream any less. All the big dreamers had someone there to assist them.

There is a woman who followed her dream of becoming a fitness bodybuilder. She is a mom of three children, and in her forties. She worked out very hard in the gym and pursued that dream with much hard work and determination. To get to the point of competition would mean many hours in a gym working on every muscle to get them into top shape. She eventually went to a national competition and placed fifth. She had brought home a trophy from that competition and now has a shirt that says *Trophy Wife*. What a great accomplishment.

It is never too late to follow a dream. Maybe you want to take a trip to a country that is far from where you live to explore another culture and see marvelous landmarks and scenery. Maybe you want to run a marathon. Maybe you want to sing in front of a crowd of ten thousand people. Maybe you want to start your own business. It is not out of reach unless you allow it to be. Many people achieve their dreams every day, and you are no different from anyone else.

When you find the pieces of who you are, you are also finding your direction. You may be following many paths to reach one destination. We still need to focus on our day to day life and then add in what we want to achieve. It is work to reach a dream. It takes dedication to pursue something that means a lot to you. You may have thought you would never achieve that dream. It was so far away that you could barely see it, but you did. All the work and effort paid off.

When following a dream, you are putting even more pieces of who you are together. You are finding the *you* that you want to be. No one can do this for you. People can help along the way, but it is you who must have the determination to reach that dream. It is you who thought of this dream and have worked so hard to make it a reality. It is you who is finding you with every step you make and every breath you take.

Sometimes a dream may take years of planning and thought until one day it all comes together. Dreams are different for everyone. If you want to go on a wonderful trip to a destination that's out of your price range, it may take a few years of planning and saving for the dream to become reality. If you want to be a singer, it may take many auditions before someone chooses you. If you want a business, it may take a few years of research, funding assistance, and market planning. If your dream is worth it, you will pursue it.

Theme parks were not built overnight. Disneyland started with a drawing on a piece of paper. It took many years for those dreams to come true, but the designers, planners, and builders did not give up. With persistence and determination, many theme parks have been created from a dream, and it is our reality to enjoy them. Now we have amazing places to feel like a kid and have a wonderful time. Those dreamers made a dream a reality. You can too.

Don't settle for a negative mindset that says you cannot achieve your dream. Don't give up if you are told you cannot do something. Keep pursuing your dream. Hold the determination in your heart. You may get bounced around a few times. You may get detours along the way. Do not let those stop you from moving forward. The detours are the routes you were meant to take. A setback is not the end. You are finding you and how determined you are when you are achieving a dream.

Do not give up on your dreams. I want you to use all your strength and not settle for less than your dream. If, however, a dream is not going to be achieved at this time, I want you to replace it. For instance, maybe your dream is to become a nurse. You have wanted to be a nurse since you were a little child. You have tried to work on this dream, but you have not been able to get college funds and are unable to carry a loan. Don't give up on your dream, but in the meantime, volunteer at your local hospital or a nursing home. Or get a job at a retirement center. It is not the dream you are pursuing exactly, but it is a stepping stone.

Sometimes the dream you choose leads you in a different direction. And that is OK too. You started out in the pursuit of one thing, but you end up reaching for something else. Maybe your dream was to be a veterinarian. You were in school to achieve your dream, but you fell in love with your art class, so you decided to become a designer instead. There is nothing wrong with a change of plans when pursuing a dream. It does not mean that you did not achieve your dream—it means you had a plan that was not meant to be and the right direction was set before you instead.

I had a dream to run a triathlon. I was not in shape, so I needed to work very hard for this to become a reality. I started working out, and I would practice at the pool where we went camping. I could lift weights and was pretty strong for a female my age. I dreamed of being the first place female triathlon competitor. This was in my younger years (high school) and it became my dream after taking a weight lifting class as an elective. I did not know how strong I was until I had taken the class and I had even impressed the football coach. I was pretty sure of myself at the time and wanted to push myself even further. I was able to run a mile on the track but I realized I was exhausted after I ran. It was hard for me and it hurt my back. Whether I hit the ground too hard with my feet or I wasn't breathing right, I am not sure, but I knew running wasn't working for me. I also found out that I love swimming in a pool, but I am not good at swimming in open water. The waves throw me off and I have a fear of not being able to swim toward the side of a pool. Well, that took away my dream of winning a triathlon.

I gave up on the dream of winning a triathlon, but it was still in my heart to do something athletic. Many years later my dad had several surgeries due to arthritis. By the age of fifty, he was in a wheelchair. Our major city sponsors an arthritis run, and I'd never known about it. After my father developed many complications with arthritis, I discovered this run. At that time, I had not been exercising regularly and was not in very good shape, but I decided a 5K was going to be my triathlon. It may not have been my original dream, but it was a dream and the best I could do. I completed my first 5K. I was not in first place. In fact, my sister teased me when I crossed the finish line because she said a seventy-year-old man had crossed the line way before I did. I didn't care. At the moment I crossed that finish line, I felt like I just won my first triathlon. I set out to do something and I did it. I finished! I achieved a dream. It may have been a second-place dream, but it was a dream. I have done a few more races since then, and I feel a sense of accomplishment every time.

Don't feel like your dreams do not matter. Don't feel that they are not big enough to be considered dreams. Many people run a 5K every morning for the military. It is nothing for them. For me, though, it is a major accomplishment, and I am proud of myself every time I do it. It

132

does matter. It matters to me. It matters to the person who finds little pieces of strength to fulfill a dream. Just because something may be easy for someone else and you have to work hard to get there, don't think your dream does not count.

Look at how many people take exotic trips every year like it is not a big deal. But the average household has to save for a couple years to take a trip like that. Just because it may be a regular occurrence for others, your dream is still your dream. Many people take their kids to Disneyland more than once in a lifetime. This may be a silly dream to most people, but one of my dreams is to take my kids to Disneyland. We had planned to go when our youngest turned five. We didn't go. When she was eight, we were getting divorced. Being a single mom, I did not have the money to take my kids to Disneyland. Now they are grown, but I am still planning on taking them. I don't care if they are thirty years old when we go—I will achieve my dream. Even if the dreams don't happen when you want them to, don't give up on them. I still pursue this dream to be there with my kids. They think it is silly, but it's very important to me, and I will keep pursuing this dream until it becomes a reality. No dream is silly. No dream is not worth pursuing.

When you accomplish something you set out to do, how does it make you feel? Do you feel happy, fulfilled? Are you surprised that you achieved it? Did you want to quit in the middle but you decided to keep going? When you accomplish a goal or dream, it is showing you what you are made of: strength and determination. The power to pursue. You discover pieces of the missing you.

You are heading in the direction you want to go when you achieve a dream. You may feel that you have been lost, but when you achieve a dream, you were always there. You may have struggled and felt like it was not worth the effort. You may have wondered why you even started trying in the first place. You may have taken a break for a while and pondered if you wanted to continue. In the end, you did not quit. You finished what you started and found many missing pieces of yourself along the way.

What is your dream? What do you want to accomplish in this lifetime? Take the chance and start acting on your dream today. The final destination may be far away, but you can start acting on it now. No dream happens overnight. Don't think it is so far off that you can't do it. Don't think it is too big to never come true. The most amazing things have happened to ordinary people. Dreams don't come true only for other people. Dreams can come true for you. Take your chance to act. Step out of your comfort zone, and take action.

Never give up on what is important to you. If it is important to you, then it is worth the pursuit. Nothing is quite like the feeling of a personal accomplishment. We achieve things every day, but when we have a special dream that takes work, it is one of the best feelings when it becomes reality. For example, consider people who have written books that turned into a series of books. That series of books has turned into a TV show or movies.

You never know where your dream will take you. It can take you places you never imagined. Find your pieces, find your determination, find your strength, and never stop reaching for your dreams.

Chapter Ten

Live in the Moment

Yesterday is gone

Tomorrow is not here

All you have is this moment

It is very precious and dear.

This moment will be a memory

Like all the others past

Live it to the fullest

Make every moment last.

Sometimes the most important moment you have may just tick away. ~td

We tend to live in the past or look forward to the future. Seldom do we ever appreciate the moment: the time that is right now. The only time we actually have. We look back on what has happened in our past and what we missed, what we should have done, what we did, what we have been through, where the time has slipped away. We look to the future of what will be next, what we plan on. The past is a good reflection on what has brought us to where we are today. Tomorrow is a time that has not taken place. We get anxious about what tomorrow may hold. We often think of the future, which keeps us from enjoying what we have right now.

At this moment, you are who you are. If you have dreams you are pursuing, small goals you want to reach, changes you want to make, or you're trying to discover your next direction, this moment will be a part of what gets you there. Each moment we have is a moment to be who we want to be. Each moment is the place you are supposed to be at that very time. For example, there is a reason that you are reading this book at this very moment. There is something in your life that needed to read some or all of these words to get you through to your future moments. Each moment is a time to be present in.

We talked about letting go of the past, discarding things that may have been hurtful or keep you from moving on. The past can also be a place of happiness that's left behind. The past could be where you wish you still were. Maybe you had a mountain of good times that you wish you were still living. It seems as if life sometimes gets more difficult and has more responsibilities. New decisions have to be made and more changes await. In the past, it was simple. We enjoyed things more and life didn't seem to be so hard. But that is the past—a romanticized view of the past, really. You are now in this moment, and this is where you can make good times happen.

Before moving to the farm, I lived in the suburbs. I can look back and think about how simple it was then. Everything was close by. I was raising my kids in a nice place, and we had many friends around us. Life seemed simple and pleasant. We had the kids' sports, went to town events, enjoyed our neighbors, and just living our daily lives. Now I live one to two hours away from friends and family. I am on five acres with woods surrounding me, so I can't just go outside and talk to neighbors. The local stores are not as close by, and it tends to feel lonely. It seems as if the past was a better place to be. Oh, wait, that's right. The past is when I was going through my divorce, stressed to no end, driving here and there and everywhere, trying to care for three kids and a house while being a super busy single mom. So how simple was it? What only our mind remembers.

We look back and see what we want to see. We can see the bad and forget about the good times, or we can see the good times and not remember the bad. We see what we want to see and remember what we want to at the moment. Remembering the past is not bad; it is just not helpful to keep yourself there.

Some people look at the past with regret, wishing they had done something differently. That is not good, either. Things happen for a reason. There is a path for each of us. We may not like the path we are currently on, but we cannot look back and dwell. You cannot change what has happened in the past. You cannot go back and make a different decision to change where you are.

I hear often that you shouldn't have any regrets. I know I have them. I believe people can have regrets, but I don't think that we should focus on them.

My regrets are about people in particular, about not spending enough time with them. I get so busy in my own life that I don't spend the time I want with family and friends. I work on changing this for my future, but I don't dwell on it. It hurts that I missed spending time with people who are important in my life. These past mistakes were not intentional. They were not even noticeable at the time. Now that I am aware, though, I know I need to make changes.

The future is also a place that can keep you from the moment. You can take your present in hand and plan for the future, as I am doing.

But do not keep looking at the future as if you wish you were there instead of focusing on where you are right now. If you have goals or changes that you want to make, you can look to the future to give yourself a mental picture of what it may be like when we reach that goal. It gives us a boost to keep moving in that direction. What you don't want to do is linger in the future wishing you were already there.

Do not worry about the future. We do not know what the future holds, though we may *think* we know. When I was planning to move out to the farm, I thought about the future all the time. I was worried about moving further away. Worried that I couldn't take care of the animals properly. Worried something bad would happen and I wouldn't know how to respond. Essentially, I worried about something that had not even happened yet.

When I look back on all that worry, I realize it was just a waste of time. Yes, we had some bad things happen. A horse got a cut in her leg. My granddaughter fell out of bed and broke her collarbone. We had a horse miscarriage. We had a tragedy with one of our dogs. But we handled them. We took care of each situation when it happened, and not once did I worry at the time that I could not do it. Things happen in life and you deal with the situation at hand.

Basically, I worried for nothing. I worried about a future that didn't even take place how I thought it would. I wasted energy and time on thoughts. Not real life, but just thoughts I had in my head. You cannot worry about something that has not happened yet. Even if you know something is set for the future, you really do not know the outcome until it happens.

Don't think of the future as your only possible happiness. I know a few people who constantly think about future events that will make them happy. Of course, you are planning a trip to a beautiful ocean, which would make you happy. That is something to look forward to. I am talking about people who think only certain events will make them happy. "I will be happy when I have my own house" or "I will happy when I finally fall in love" or "I will happy when I find a new job."

We do not know what the future holds. We don't know when or if these events will take place. We don't know if these events will change the status of our happiness. Be happy in the moment. Do not wait to find happiness.

What is happening at this moment in your life, besides reading this book? Are there kids sleeping soundly in the other room? Is there a nice fire going to comfort you from the cold? Is there a dog lying at your side? Are you in the city and reading by the light of outside life? Take these moments and look around you and see what is taking place. This is the moment you are in. This is where you are right now. You are not in the past, and you are not in the future. You are right here, right now. Take in this moment. Feel it. Each moment is a time that is given to us. We can choose what we feel in each of our moments. Are you feeling happy where you are? Are you sad about something? Are you anxious? Are you content? What are feeling this very moment?

Accept where you are right now. Acceptance is the key to living in the moment. Accept that what has happened in the past has brought you to where you are right now. Accept that you do not know what the future holds but that you will continue to move forward. Accept that you are where you need to be at this moment. Everything has happened for a reason to get you to where you are, and things will continue to happen to get you to where you need to be. Enjoy where you are.

I have been through many tough situations. At times I did not want to be where I was. I wanted to fast forward my life a few weeks. But as you know, that is not possible. You have to endure what you are given, even in times of trial. Even though I wanted to fast forward, I still took each moment and appreciated it. For one, I was alive. I was breathing, and I still had life in me to get through another moment of time. I also had and still have a strong will. Although I don't like going through tough times, I find out more about myself through each one. I appreciate every moment I have because it brings me to a place I like to be.

If you are in a difficult situation right now, don't wish your way out. Look to the future as a goal of where you want to be. Get a mental image of where you are heading. Use your moments to get you there. Wishing it away will not take it away. Using your moments to find solutions is what will get you out of the situation. If you don't have enough money to get from one paycheck to the next, use your moment to look for a new job or an additional one. If you are in a bad relationship, take these moments to plan for a way to end it. If you are unhappy with your current situation, take these moments to find out what will make you feel better. These are your moments to use. Do not waste them. Enjoy them. Appreciate every moment. It is one more moment you have at being you. It is one more moment you have to fulfill a dream. It is one more moment you have to find you.

The concept of living in the moment has been around for many years. Many cultures focus on this as a way of life, but it is difficult for most of us to live this way. We are always in such a hurry to get things done that we tend to focus on what is next. What do we have to get done by 5pm? What do we have to do on our way home? What do I need for that party next week? We need to stop and look at where we are and what we feel, and take the moment and appreciate it.

I want you to try something: sit down and look at the moment you are in. Close your eyes. Closing your eyes will bring you to yourself. Take a few moments to feel. Feel your emotions, feel your breathing, feel your body just sitting there. Appreciate this moment you have. Let it be your moment because it really does belong only to you. This is your time to be you. You do not have to do anything for anyone else. You don't have to run to the store for milk. You don't have to plan for a meeting at work. You don't have to worry about what will happen tomorrow. You don't have to do anything. This is your moment to appreciate you and who you are. This is your moment to feel who you are right now, where you are at in your life. Don't think about anything negative. Don't worry, don't be sad, and don't be fearful. Be happy. You were given this time to be you, and you need to take the moments to appreciate who you are.

When you block out the surroundings around you, all you have left to focus on is you. And this is what this book is all about. YOU! Finding you. Finding the direction you are supposed to be heading. When you take time to just be with yourself, you will find more pieces that you may have been missing. The busy world outside of those closed eyes does not exist. Only you exist. This allows you time to take a closer look at yourself from a different view. You are not looking in a mirror, you have no work title, you are not just another person in traffic. You are just you for who you are. The real person taking a moment in life to appreciate your existence. Take these moments. Live in these moments. There is no past; there is no future. There is only right now.

Be happy to just be you. There is no one else like you. You are unique. You are special in your own way. Take the moment to know who you are. When you open your eyes and continue throughout your day, keep notice of your moments and live them. They are not just time ticking away: they are moments of your life. They are now. They are the only true time you have and the only real time you are living. Keep yourself in the present time. Enjoy each moment that is given to you.

I have a lot to look forward to in my future. I have a husband who I have been married to but have not lived with. We were dating when he was stationed in Guam. When I decided to move to the farm, he did propose to me, but we had not lived together. When I moved over to his house, he was there for a week to show me the ins and outs of making the place functional. It was a quick teaching session and we didn't have time to really think of anything other than what I needed to know and getting his belongings packed. Along with this, I was preparing my home for tenants to move in, painting walls, cleaning carpets, and making sure I had everything moved out in time. Then he was gone. Just like that.

We will be married for two years before we get to live together as husband and wife. He also now has new orders to another state. I can think about the future and worry or I can live in the moment. I do try to plan for the future, but I am not focusing all of my attention there. I know changes are coming. I know life will be different. I know I may be moving out of state for the first time in my life. I will finally get to have my husband with me and live a life together. It is something I look forward to and try to plan for but until the time comes, I am here right now. I have the responsibilities of the farm, my job, my family, and my life. I focus on what I need to do now, at this time, to plan for the new life ahead of me. I am taking steps now so when the future comes I am better prepared. I don't know what the future will be. I just know at this moment what is planned for it. But I live for now.

Remember when I said the past is a learning experience? I worried about moving out to the farm, but I learned from my experience. Worrying was a waste of time and energy. I will not do this the next time. I know the basics: I know my husband will be coming home to visit, I know he will be going to another state, and I know I will have a major life change. I know I will then live with my husband. I get excited about being with my husband, but until then, I live in the moments that I have. Because this is really all I have.

As you move on, don't live in your past. It is gone and does not exist any longer. Do not live in the future—it has not happened. Live this very moment that you have right now. Appreciate it. Accept it. Be you.

Chapter Eleven

Believe in a Higher Power

Is there something more

That we cannot see

That takes us through our days?

That guides us, surrounds us

Leads us to a path

And helps us to find our way?

It's not always about believing in something you have to see. ~td

There are many different religions and beliefs. Some people believe that there is a Higher Power, and some people believe we just live on this earth and pass away to nothing. Some people believe that if there was a Higher Power, It would not let bad things happen. Some people believe religion is a cult. Some people believe it is an excuse to not live in the real world. I personally believe that there is a Higher Power: God and the son, Jesus Christ.

I have friends who believe differently, but I do not judge them for their beliefs and they do not judge me for mine. I do not believe that everything happens to us by chance; I believe a plan is set out for us and we are making our way through it. I also believe that life happens, and just because bad things happen, it does not mean there is no God. Earth is a place of living; it is not meant to be all goodness, sweetness, and roses. Heaven is where you will find eternal peace. Good and evil exist on Earth, and it is in our life trials that we find who we are in this world. God did not say there would be no trials, even for those who believe. It says in *James 1:2-3 My brethren, count it all joy when you fall into various trials, knowing that the testing of your faith produces patience.*

Bad things will happen to good people. It may not seem fair or right, but it is life. Have you seen on the news when a person is being tried for murder and a mom of the victim forgives the person? That is an image of a Higher Power and faith. Instead of hating, yelling, and blaming, they cry and let the murderer know that they are forgiven. It does not mean they are not hurt and aching inside or that they will forget what has happened. It means they are forgiving the act. Forgiving is not a sign of weakness; it's a sign of ultimate strength, the hardest thing a person can do. People forgive because they do not want to carry the burden of hatred and they want to free their heart of anger and bitterness. I believe they get this strength from their Higher Power.

Some people get angry at God for bad things that happen to them, thinking God doesn't love them. That is not true. God does love you. There may have been a lesson in life that needed to be learned, and a trial was the way of making you see it. Maybe life took you on this path, and the path could have been so much worse, but it was God who kept you from something more devastating. We don't have the answers. We don't know why things happen the way they do, but I do believe there are reasons we may not understand that are putting us on a path we are meant to follow.

Many years ago, I was driving down a highway at 50 mph. My ex-husband was in the passenger seat, and my three young children were in the backseat. I was driving a Dodge Ram Charger, which is similar to a full-size Bronco. The road was a two-lane highway and ran through a wooded area. There were only a few turn-offs on this road. I was driving behind a large van that had put on its blinker to veer into a left turn lane. I had misjudged the distance of the turn lane and started to move around the van so I wouldn't have to slow down. When I looked, the van was still a distance away from the turn lane and I was moving up to the side of it. This was my mistake. It was a common practice on this road, but the van was far from the turn lane, and I made the mistake of going around him. I hit a small drop-off on the pavement and hit the dirt on the side of the road. The right side of the Ram went up a small embankment and tipped the truck up. The next thing I remember the Ram bounced back onto the road right next to the van and was only inches away. I could have touched the van with my hand out the window, it was so close. The van slowed down and made the left hand turn, and my vehicle continued to move forward. I was in shock at what just happened, and when I came back to reality, I grabbed the steering wheel and continued to drive.

I think this was the most frightened my ex-husband had ever been. He said, "I cannot believe we didn't just roll the truck. I can't believe you got out of that."

I was still looking ahead and responded, "Did you see how close we came to the van? I should have hit it."

As he was still holding the rail by the door, he continued stating that we should have died. I was still looking ahead. I could not believe what had happened. It was not the fact that we almost just had a terrible accident—it was something more.

"I don't think I got us out of that," I said.

My ex-husband looked at me puzzled. He knows that we just missed a large accident, and I am saying I didn't get us out of that, yet I am the one driving. "What do you mean you didn't get us out of that? You just did."

He didn't understand what I was saying. I told him it wasn't me. I don't remember turning the wheel or doing anything. I just remember sitting in the driver's seat watching it all take place. I did not respond to anything. It was like the truck was driving itself. He must have thought I was a little crazy at that point, but it was true. In any other driving situation where an accident may have occurred such as someone turning in front of me, cutting me off in a lane, or swerving in my lane, I had responded. At those times I remember checking mirrors, moving quickly, turning the wheel, putting on brakes. In this situation, I did none of that. It felt like someone or something else took over the vehicle and got us to safety.

I will never forget that moment. It has been twenty years since that almost-accident. I still do not recall taking any actions to remove us from that bad situation. Was it an angel? I don't know. I just know it was not me, and there was a Higher Power involved. I know people tend to forget something bad or don't recall something when a difficult moment is taking place. I remember watching everything. I was just not responding. It was not me behind the wheel for those few seconds.

Life has many courses, some good and some bad. Some we can avoid if we listen to our inner voice. Some happen due to our choices and some happen because it was meant to be. I am not immune to the bad in the world, and I have had many trials, some worse than what other people endure and some that are a cakewalk compared to what others have had to go through.

I am human like anyone else, and I hurt when I see a missing child notice. My heart is saddened for the parents and I can't image what it would be like for them. I ache when I see a shooting spree and people dying at the hands of another person. I mourn when there is a natural disaster and so many lives are taken. I wonder why. I believe God does not make bad things happen, but He does allow them. There are reasons behind a tragedy that we will not understand, but I do not lose my faith. In a horrible situation, I thank God for those who survived. I pray a child is found. I pray for the responders and thank God for caring people who help in these situations.

I have seen tragic occurrences, and I often hear, "We just thank God that we are alive." These people could be full of hatred and bitterness about what just happened in their lives and blame God for it. Instead they are thanking Him. It is all how you feel about a Higher Power. Some people say belief is weakness, that people need to believe in something to get through life because they cannot do it on their own. But I think that belief is strength and courage to embrace something that is not visually seen. Is there anything wrong with that? Is it hurting anyone else believing there is something more to this existence than just what is on earth? As long as they are not using their beliefs to hurt other people, no, I see nothing wrong with it. Something to believe in is a good thing.

Miracles happen every day. There are things in our world that we cannot explain. The medical profession has seen many miracles. Doctors treating a patient sometimes think the only outcome is death, yet some people miraculously heal with no medical or scientific explanation. And there are tragedies in which everyone in the situation should have perished, yet some people live. If we as humans cannot explain these with all the knowledge and technology we have, then what caused these miracles? I believe it is the Higher Power. Through tragedy there is light. Through bad there is good.

We do not have the answers for everything, although we would like to. Until we pass from this earth, we do not know. I don't want to wait till the end to find out I did not believe in something that was there all along. If I get to the end and there is nothing, I had a great belief system along the way. I am not telling you what you should believe in; I am sharing my belief only because it has helped me in my life. If you are feeling like you are missing something, a Higher Power may be what you need. When you are lonely, God can be your friend. Although He is not here in the physical, He is with you always in spirit. He will listen to you. Guide you. Hold you when you are weak and bless you into a fulfilling life.

I have been through many trials. I don't blame God for them. I pray to Him and ask Him to give me strength, for the will to get through, for safety as I walk in a path that may be dangerous. I know I will only be given what I can handle. I often think God may have forgotten about how much I have already endured, and a break from stress and tribulations would be nice, but I still lean on Him. They say when you go through a tough time it is because there is something better waiting for you at the end. We do not always see it right away, but it is there. When I look back

156

on where I was and what I have been through, I always found something better than before. When a door closed and I was pounding to get back in, I didn't look to see what other door was opening for me. Once that door was discovered, it was much better than the door that was closed behind me.

I also thank God for what I have. I don't have a never-ending checking account, but I have what I need and I am very blessed to have it. I am rich with people in my life who love me. I am rich with being who I am and rich because I have a Higher Power who loves me unconditionally. I thank Him for the way my life is going, trials and all. I thank Him for my wonderful children, and I am blessed to be their mom. If you do believe in the Higher Power, don't always go to Him when you want something. Don't keep asking Him for things. Thank Him for what you do have. Thank Him for giving you opportunities in life. Thank Him for having one more day on earth. Thank Him for everything. We may not always get what we want. Some prayers are not meant to be answered.

Believe the path you are on is a plan the Higher Power designed to get you to a better place. We are here to exceed and evolve in life, not be stagnant. We are meant to better ourselves and succeed. Believe the plan is set for you to be better. You may have difficult times during this pathway and a few turns you don't want to take, but the path will still lead you in the right direction. Have faith. Just because you cannot see it, does not mean it is not there.

The Higher Power has much to offer us on earth. He will help us when the load gets too much to bear. We talked earlier about letting go of hurts and pains that are keeping us from moving forward. If you are having a hard time letting go, give it to God. Let Him take it from you. We are given what we can handle, but we are not meant to carry it around with us once we go through it. Sometimes we need help to move on.

Have you heard the expression "Let go and let God?" My grandma gave us girls a little stained-glass window decal with that saying. I was younger and didn't understand it at the time. As I got older, I got more stubborn and independent. I thought I could take on anything. But there came a point in my life I had to let go and give it to God. I was carrying a burden; I was not letting go of a life situation.

I mentioned before that my son had some difficult years. He was thirteen when his dad left the home. A boy at that age needs his dad. It was a tough time for my son, and he acted out in negative ways. He got in trouble at school, skipped classes, and abused drugs and alcohol. And I was in denial of it all. He was home when I got home. He was home when I went to bed. He was there when I got up in the morning. I never saw him do anything wrong, so I didn't believe that he was in trouble. He managed to hide it well, and as a mom, I don't know how I missed the signs. Eventually he ended up in the court system due to an arrest. I actually watched my son at fifteen years old be arrested on my front lawn. He'd vandalized a new school being built in our city by spraying fire extinguishers in the building and wrapping caution tape around the poles under construction, which is illegal.

He went to jail for a few hours, and I had to pick him up at 2:00 am. We started going to drug counseling. I was trying to handle my son's situations while still looking after his two younger sisters and keeping them in their sports and regular activities. It was a challenging time. I tried everything I could think of with my son. He was never abusive or angry towards me. He was just lying and having a life I did not ever see, and I was trying to stop it. His dad at this time was working out of state and was not helping with the situation, so it was all on me. I had to miss work for court dates, plus I had to cancel things I wanted to do so I could attend his treatments, and I was getting little sleep. I was praying every night for things to get better. I was praying that he would stop what he was doing and get on the right path. I was praying for the safety of him, my daughters, and me due to the fights he was getting in. I was praying for everything and it was not getting better, and I could not understand why my prayers were not being answered.

The last thing that happened took me to a place where I knew I could not carry this burden any longer. My son was sixteen and had been drinking. He was very ill and acting very strange. We were in my car to go to his friend's house and get his backpack, and I wanted to find out what he had been drinking since he was acting so bizarre. He got out of the car and began to vomit foam. I was terrified. I knew my son was on probation and would be in trouble if he'd drunk alcohol. But I was worried for his life, so I called 911. The medics came and took him to the hospital. He was fine and released, but I was done. I realized I was praying for all of these things, but I wasn't giving God a chance to act on them. I was controlling the situation on my end. I was praying for God to help but I would not let go and let Him. I finally prayed and said, "Lord, I cannot do this any longer. I am not doing well here and I need to give it to You. Do what You need to do. I know You will do what is right and I don't want to lose my son. I know You will do what needs to be done to make this better. I give it to You, Lord. Please take this from me. I release it to You."

You can call it coincidence or a fluke, but in the months to come, my son started to heal. He started to make the right choices in his life. He started to take on responsibilities. He was coming back to me as the boy I raised. I had tried everything in my power and nothing had worked. It was after I gave it to God that things started to change. Not right away, but in slow and steady paces. My son is a hardworking, responsible father, husband, and supporter now. Some of those friends he hung around back then have not found their way. My son stepped out on his own and found his. I know it was a Higher Power that stepped in and handled this situation for me. It was a Higher Power that saved him.

We can think these things happen by luck or by chance. We can think there is nothing else other than the earth and that which we see. I believe there is something more that we cannot see. I have experiences that I cannot explain, and I feel blessed to have experienced them. I feel that God is there every step of the way, and I believe I get through difficult situations in life because I have the Higher Power guiding me. If you feel that something is missing in your life, believe in the Higher Power and let Him guide you. Ask for His help. Thank Him for what you have. Even in trials thank Him, because you know He is leading you to something better. I know I will continue to believe in what is not seen yet still has a bigger existence than Earth itself.

You can get through life not believing in a Higher Power. People do it all the time. But when you do believe, your life has a different meaning. It has more quantity and fulfillment. I am not talking about material fulfillment. I'm talking about the inside. Let Him be in your life and acknowledge that He is making the correct pathway for you. My favorite Bible verse that gets me through many situations: *Philippians 4:13, I can do all things through Christ who strengthens me.*

Chapter Twelve

Here all Along

I have not lost myself

I just lost my way

Took a different path

That led me to today.

Now I know my direction

I know which way to go

Always stepping forward

Always discovering more.

What you set out to seek may be the one thing you didn't have to find. ~td

We have been through eleven chapters of finding you. The missing person you have been trying to find has been here all along. You have been where you need to be. Right here. You were not lost; you were just heading in the wrong direction. Now it is the time to get on the right path and move forward. Now is the time to discover a new world that is waiting for you. Now is the time to take your first steps beyond the past, beyond your comfort zone, and enjoy every moment that leads you into your future. Let's recap what we have discussed.

You made a list of values. Keep that list handy to remind you of what is important in your life. Take time to focus on your values and keep them active in your daily life. Do not let people or objects take you away from your values. Your values are a part of who you are. We tend to lose sight of our values when we let life take over. Be in control of your life. Enjoy what is important to you. Your values may change. That is fine as long as you are still enjoying them and bringing them into your daily life. When things change in our life, our values may change too. Whatever your values are at any point in your life, appreciate them and take time for what is important to you.

Toxic people can contribute to how we feel about ourselves and where we are going. The negative impact these people can have may make you wonder about yourself and who you really are. Toxic people need to be removed or minimized in your life. You should be confident in yourself to stand up against the emotions toxic people may bring to the surface. If they are pulling energy from you and they are not lifting you, then keep them at a distance. It is not that they are bad people; they are just not right for you. You should have people around you that lift your spirits, make you feel good about yourself, and bring joy to your life. Do not let toxic people take any pieces away from you. You are who you are. You cannot please everyone, but you can please yourself. You now know who is toxic in your life and you will know in the future what to look for. Keep yourself from negative people and associate with positive ones. Fill your social ring with energy that makes you exhausted only because you were having so much fun.

Losing love hurts. Our heart hurts and we want to eat lots of ice cream and stay in bed for days. Maybe at first we will do that, but then we must keep moving forward. We need to pick ourselves up and wipe away those tears. Learn from the relationship and what worked and what didn't. Take the experience with you to the next relationship. Not all relationships are meant to last. The one that does will be because of everything you learned on the way. When you're alone, appreciate that time. Take that time for you. Don't be on the hunt to get the next relationship, but take some time in between to focus back on you, your values, and your goals.

This is a time to be happy about you and what you want in life. When the time is right, you will enter into a relationship more fulfilled and ready to share this wonderful person called you.

We cannot take all the stress away from our lives, but we can be responsible for how we respond to it and find the little things we can control during stressful times. Do not let stress consume you. Know that it is a regular part of life and it will be less of a burden to you when you take a breath, focus on the situation, and control the things you can. Your attitude and your strength will get you through. Make choices that will benefit you. Take this time as a challenge that you will overcome in a positive way. Focus on what you can control and let that be your guide. Take some deep breaths, relax, and know stress is an emotion. You can take control over it. You are strong and you will get through. When you do, celebrate. Have fun, take a load off, and enjoy life.

Be positive! Life may not always go as you planned, but that is no reason to be down and out. Look at the good in what happened and what is happening now. Your attitude will make or break it. We can focus on the bad, but where is that going to get us? Pretty much two steps back and then one step forward again. Be positive about where you are and where you will be going. There is so much to life, and just because a moment may be bad, doesn't mean the next five moments will be. The energy you produce is how situations will continue to be. When you are looking toward the good, you will be lead there. It is all about the choices you make and what you choose to feel. Feel the good! You never know where it will lead you.

Let the past stay in the past and let it go! Stop carrying all the baggage. Lighten the load and move forward to better things. You can choose to be weighed down and be a victim, or you can be a survivor and start enjoying your time. Take what has been negative in your life and turn it into a positive. Only you are carrying the weight. Only you are choosing not to leave it behind. This is your time to drop it off, walk away, and leave it. Get a bounce in your step from taking that weight off your shoulders. Find new and great adventures to keep you moving forward. Pain is not a comfort zone you want to stay in. Step out of your box, take another step, and keep on going. Enjoy this life and enjoy you.

You are the only you. You are unique to this world. You are the only person you will be with at all times for this entire life. Love who you are. Love that you have qualities others don't have. Love that you are you! Don't focus at the bad qualities you may have, and don't compare yourself to others. Don't look down on who you are. Sure, you may want to change some things, and that is OK, but love who you are now and love who you are during the process. Don't let the outside world make you become unsure of yourself. You know you more than anyone else does. Love *you*! You are the best friend you will ever have.

Go with the changes that life will give you. Don't fight them. Don't be negative. Find the good in the change and know it was just steering you in the direction you needed to go. Life is full of changes. Nothing stays the same. Control what you can and focus on where you are now going. Your attitude will determine how these changes will affect you. Changes can be as minor as a new policy at work or a major life change. The change is leading you where you need to go. You may not like it and you may be disappointed, but hang in there, because better things are coming your way. Fear is only an emotion. Don't let fear control the changing situation. You can control fear and show it that you are strong and intend to come out better on the other side. Go with it and enjoy the new path. It will lead you to new adventures.

Write down that dream you have been thinking about but have been putting off. Start today to make that dream a reality. What if Walt Disney had never created Mickey Mouse? That one dream turned into many others, too. If you have to alter a dream, that is OK. The key is to reach for your dreams and don't underestimate your dream or yourself. Dreamers don't live in reality? Dreamers *make* our reality. Dreamers are the ones building their reality while others sit back and watch and wonder why it isn't them. Take the step. Take the chance. Your one dream can take you to places you never dreamed of.

This moment is the only moment that is real. Live in your moments. Take your moments in with positive energy. Know that where you are at this very moment is where you are meant to be. Enjoy what you have right now. Later on, you may have less and you may have more, but right now enjoy what is here. Don't live in the past. It is done. Don't try to live in the future. It is not here. Reach for your dreams, keep moving forward, strive for your future goals, but enjoy every moment during this time. These moments will pass and become memories. Don't wait to start tomorrow. Don't wait for things to come. Be right where you are and take it in. Every moment in our lives count.

Is it by chance or luck? Is this world all we have? Let a Higher Power into your life and see what you have been missing. Let Him guide you and comfort you. Let Him lead you to your destination. When obstacles cross your way, let Him be there to help you through. When you are feeling lonely, talk to Him and know you are not alone. This world has good and evil. It is not the Higher Power making bad things happen, so seek Him and let Him get you through difficult times. *Romans 12:21 Do not be overcome by evil, but overcome evil with good.* He will bless those who believe and bring Him into their lives. Angels are all around us.

Sometimes the angel is one person who gives you a smile when you are sad and need to feel like someone cares. When you are being challenged and feeling fear, remember this: *Psalm 56:3 Whenever I am afraid, I will trust in You.*

You were never lost. You have been here all along. Don't let the outside world throw you off your course. Trust yourself. You are always where you are meant to be at any given moment. You may not like every situation. Times may be hard to bear and you may want to go curl up in a ball and hide until they pass. But you can get through it. You have strength you didn't know you had until you needed to be strong. You are a special person. Unique. The past leads you to your future. You can dwell and stay in the past or you can keep on moving. You can be sad and bitter or you can be happy. These are choices. If what you want does not come to you, go out and get it. It wasn't a matter of losing who you are. It is a matter of choices. How you respond to life situations determines where you will be going. Make sure it is always forward.

Be happy. Be alive. Be a better you every day. The choice is yours. You have more control over your life than you give yourself credit for. We will have many challenges in our life. When we think it is all calm, something will come and throw it off course. The more you fight change, the more you miss out on exciting things coming your way. You have learned much.

I am so happy you took the time to value yourself enough to reach out and discover yourself in a different light. Each piece we put together makes life more exciting. We will continue to find pieces with each step we take, each moment we breathe. You were not lost. You just needed to put some pieces back in place and find new pieces along the path. Find your direction and keep walking.

At the beginning, you wrote down why you felt lost. It is time to grab that list. Do not open that piece of paper. Do not read it. Throw it away. It does not apply to you. You are not lost. You are here. You are moving in the right direction.

"You travel along with your morals and your values and become the person you think you want to be and who you don't want to be. And somewhere along the path you lose yourself. Your morals, your values, who you were and become someone you never thought. You do things you never would have done a year or two ago. But along the traveling path you finally find out exactly the person you want to be and have no limits to who you become. And even though sometimes you might lose the person you were, you are finding yourself." ~ Jessica Bernetskie

171

From the author:

Born and raised in the beautiful Pacific Northwest, I have experienced much in life as have many other people in this wonderful world. Sharing what I know to help others get through this life in a positive way and enjoy what life has to offer. I have lived in the greater Seattle area my entire life until recently. I am now living on the east coast while my husband finishes out his long term Naval career. I have three terrific children who still reside back home and two step children in two other states. They are all grown and starting their own lives. I also have three granddaughters who are rays of light in our lives. My wonderful husband has served our country in the United States Navy for 27 years. Our children who reside with us are all now furry children. We have four dogs, three horses and two mini potbelly pigs.

The first book, Finding You and Your Direction, will help you "find" yourself if you feel lost or just give you a little push in the right direction. More books will be on the way and this book is a great place to start. Some may call it self help, I call it friendly advice. At times we feel alone in this world and sometimes a friend is all you need to get through. Some are things you may know and have forgot or it could just be a little motivation to help you get yourself together and get going to where you want to be heading. A little friendly shove is a good thing!

I am happy to share inspiration with you and look forward to a wonderful future together!

Best Wishes~

Toni